REAGAN'S
GOD AND
COUNTRY

A President's Moral Compass:
His Beliefs on God, Religious Freedom,
the Sanctity of Life, and More

Regal

From Gospel Light
Ventura, California, U.S.A.

PUBLISHED BY REGAL BOOKS
FROM GOSPEL LIGHT
VENTURA, CALIFORNIA, U.S.A.
PRINTED IN THE U.S.A.

Regal Books is a ministry of Gospel Light, a Christian publisher dedicated to serving the local church. We believe God's vision for Gospel Light is to provide church leaders with biblical, user-friendly materials that will help them evangelize, disciple and minister to children, youth and families.

It is our prayer that this Regal book will help you discover biblical truth for your own life and help you meet the needs of others. May God richly bless you.

For a free catalog of resources from Regal Books/Gospel Light, please call your Christian supplier or contact us at 1-800-4-GOSPEL *or* www.regalbooks.com.

Originally published by Servant Publications in 2000.

Cover design by Left Coast Design, Portland, Oregon
Cover photograph © Corbis. Used by permission.

Library of Congress Cataloging-in-Publication Data

Freiling, Tom.
  Reagan's God and country : a president's moral compass : his beliefs on God, religious freedom, the sanctity of life, and more / Tom Freiling.
    p. cm.
  Originally published: Ann Arbor, Mich. : Vine Books, c2000.
  ISBN 0-8307-3479-1
  1. Reagan, Ronald—Religion. 2. Reagan, Ronald—Quotations. 3. Reagan, Ronald—Oratory. 4. United States—Moral conditions. 5. United States—Politics and govern-ment—Philosophy. 6. Social values—United States. 7. Political oratory—United States. I. Title.
  E877.2.F73 2004
  973.927'092—dc22   2004017043

2 3 4 5 6 7 8 9 10 11 12 13 14 15 / 12 11 10 09 08 07 06 05

Rights for publishing this book in other languages are contracted by Gospel Light World-wide, the international nonprofit ministry of Gospel Light. Gospel Light Worldwide also provides publishing and technical assistance to international publishers dedicated to producing Sunday School and Vacation Bible School curricula and books in the languages of the world. For additional information, visit www.gospellightworldwide.org; write to Gospel Light Worldwide, P.O. Box 3875, Ventura, CA 93006; or send an e-mail to info@gospellightworldwide.org.

To Nancy

CONTENTS

PREFACE

Good Friday, 1981

President Ronald Wilson Reagan was recovering comfortably in his private quarters, upstairs in the White House, when he received a visit from J. Terence Cooke, the Catholic Cardinal of the Archdiocese of New York. Cardinal Cooke was there at Reagan's request for prayer and spiritual counsel. Although he was still tired from undergoing extensive surgery, Reagan was eager to get back on his feet. But he confided to a friend that before resuming work at the Oval Office, he desired to pray with a religious leader. Reagan was perplexed at having been "spared" and wanted to discuss it with a minister or priest.

He had been president for only nine weeks when, on March 30, 1981, John W. Hinkley Jr. attempted to take Reagan's life. On a sidewalk outside the Washington Hilton, one of six bullets Hinkley fired in rapid succession bounced freakishly off the President's motorcade, struck him under his left arm, and stopped less than an inch from his heart. Captured live on camera, it's a scene etched in the memories of the American public. Reagan had obviously been hit. But, at first, Reagan thought he had broken a rib when thrown into the backseat of his limousine by Secret Service agent Jerry Parr. Reagan shares what happened next in his memoirs:

> I tried to sit up on the edge of the seat and was almost paralyzed by pain. As I was straightening up, I had to cough hard and saw that the palm of my hand was brimming with

extremely red, frothy blood ... Suddenly, I realized I could barely breathe. No matter how hard I tried, I couldn't get enough air.

Soon he—and the world—would understand the seriousness of his injury. Parr directed the driver to speed to George Washington Hospital instead of the White House. Reagan became confused and next found himself on a gurney. He had lost half of his blood. Nurses had trouble finding his pulse. As he struggled to breathe and lay half-conscious in the hospital emergency room, the ominous likelihood that he might not survive became all too real. "I was frightened and started to panic," recounts Reagan, and for good reason. Benjamin Aaron, the surgeon who operated on him, said he was "right on the margin of death." He was on the verge of joining the grim ranks of Lincoln and Kennedy.

But instead Reagan would become the first American president not to perish from a wound in an assassination attempt. He not only survived the harrowing experience, but did so with wit and poise. On the way to the operating table, he told his wife Nancy, "I forgot to duck." And just before he was anesthetized, he quipped to the surgeon, "I hope you're a Republican." The American people were endeared by his heroic performance, which set the stage for a sudden rise in his public persona and a series of legislative victories.

But now, only two weeks after Reagan's brush with death, he was less triumphant and more reflective about the experience. Left alone with his thoughts, Reagan probably contemplated the same sort of ethereal things anyone would who had barely escaped a sudden death. Maybe he wondered about eternity and the afterlife, or possibly he thought about his childhood, his devout mother, or his early days in church. Or maybe he pondered one of the many Scripture verses he had memorized in his youth, but had long since forgotten. We don't know for certain what Ronald Reagan had been thinking in the days after he almost died, but we do know that he recollected the horrible events with Cardinal Cooke. Cooke said Reagan was somewhat mystified as to the purpose for his living through the ordeal. Cardinal Cooke assured the convalescing president that "the hand of God was upon you." "I know," replied Reagan, "and whatever time He's left for me is His." Reagan retold this peculiar testimony, that God had saved him for a unique destiny, to other religious leaders as well, including Billy Graham, Mother Teresa, and southern California pastor Donn Moomaw.

In the months following the assassination attempt, Reagan continued to convey a renewed sense of Divine Providence to other friends and family members. Pollster Richard Wirthin recounts a discussion he had with Reagan shortly after the president returned from the hospital. "The thing that he told me," said Wirthin, "was that he felt very close to passing through the portal of death and that he was spared, if you will, because there was something the Lord wanted him to accomplish." The world might construe Reagan's words to have been just a well-mannered response to congenial clergymen and concerned friends. But a closer look reveals that Reagan's reaction to the attempt on his life was more than just an affable pleasantry, but rather an introspective, heartfelt expression of how deeply he believed God had saved his life for a special purpose. Since his childhood, Reagan had believed God was involved in directing the events of human history. He often spoke of how George Washington's prayers had led to miraculous victories on the battlefields of New England; how Abraham Lincoln had steeped himself in the Bible during the most dire days of the Civil War; how Winston Churchill had reached out to God for help during the darkest days of the Second World War. "You can call it mysticism if you want to," said Reagan, "but I have always believed that there was some divine plan that placed this great continent between two oceans to be sought out by those who were possessed of an abiding love of freedom and a special kind of courage." Now he saw his surviving an assassin's bullet as a part of God's plan.

Reagan summed up his feelings about the assassination attempt in his diary. "God, for some reason," he wrote, "had seen fit to give me his blessing and allow me to live awhile longer.... Whatever happens now I owe my life to God and will try to serve him in every way I can." At age seventy, Reagan's nearly dying deepened the meaning of his faith in God, and his faith in God's plan for his life. Aide William Norton Smith observed, "I think Reagan emerged from that whole period of his life more convinced than ever that he was doing God's work...."

Reagan's reaction to the near-fatal attempt on his life illustrated an important juncture in his approach to God and public service. It wasn't, however, the first time Reagan had brought God into the mix of his private life and public career. He was already, in fact, one of the most religious presidents in American history.

Billy Graham once said that Ronald Reagan's legacy is not just political, but spiritual. "His emphasis on moral and spiritual values was one of his greatest contributions," wrote Graham in January 1997. Graham said Reagan "made Americans feel good about themselves" and "pointed them to the moral and spiritual foundations which have made this nation great—foundations derived from the biblical Judeo-Christian heritage."

Indeed, Ronald Reagan spoke and wrote much about prayer and patriots, faith and sacrifice, the flag and the Bible, morality and freedom. Using the office of president as his "bully pulpit," he devoted hundreds of discourses to religious themes—more than any other president in the twentieth century. One study by Berkeley professor William Ker Muir Jr. revealed that in one year alone, 1983, almost one-tenth of all his prepared remarks were religious in nature. In contrast, Reagan's predecessor, Jimmy Carter, himself a self-professed born-again Christian and Sunday school teacher, gave only a handful of addresses to religious audiences as president and publicly discussed the topic of religion in a substantive manner only a few times. Reagan's religious reflections weren't only verbal, but written as well. He was the first American president to write a book while holding the office of president. In *Abortion and the Conscience of the Nation*, he, C. Everett Koop, M.D., surgeon general of the United States, and Malcolm Muggeridge, the celebrated British Christian journalist, proclaimed that "prayer and action are needed to uphold the sanctity of human life."

Not since Lincoln had a sitting president addressed spiritual and moral issues as frequently as Reagan did. Like Lincoln, who relied on the Bible and Judeo-Christian principles to defend the abolitionists, Reagan relied on the same to oppose communism and the spread of secularism in American culture and abroad. "The Almighty has his own purposes," proclaimed Lincoln in his second inaugural address, and "whatever shall appear to be God's will I will do," as he emancipated the slaves.

Similarly, Reagan expressed the same conviction throughout his public career.

Yet, despite the prominent place religion played in the Reagan presidency, there's a conspicuous void in substantive commentary and literature about Reagan's religious reflections. Reagan's biographers—official and unofficial—journalists, and political commentators write about it either sparingly or disparagingly. Edmund Morris, Reagan's official biographer, makes only oblique references to Reagan's strong positions on issues as abortion and school prayer.

In his book, *President Reagan: The Role of a Lifetime,* Lou Cannon says Reagan was "more curious about biblical portents than about governmental processes," but then calls little attention to the role of prayer in Reagan's life, or to Reagan's astute knowledge of Scripture. Instead he focuses on supposed "strange" religious experiences, and on Reagan's "preoccupation" with nuclear holocaust and biblical Armageddon. Simon and Schuster's *Encyclopedia of the American Presidency* makes no mention of Reagan's religiosity. In preparing to compile and edit this book, I scoured hundreds of newspaper, magazine, and journal articles, but could find only a handful that discuss how Reagan's religious beliefs affected his approach to leadership. Perhaps only Dinesh D'Souza, former senior domestic policy analyst in the Reagan White House, gives the topic a fair assessment in his seminal book, *Ronald Reagan: How an Ordinary Man Became an Extraordinary Leader.* D'Souza leaves little room for dispute about the "sincerity of his deep faith in God and his acceptance of·the fundamental truths of Christianity."

Apparently, many historians who fill our bookshelves with their political commentaries want to avoid discussing Reagan's spiritual legacy. It's a side of Reagan that secularists might prefer to forget. To the secular elite—the pundits, historians, and university professors—Reagan's spiritual pretenses were sheer nonsense. He was a simpleton, casting himself in the role of a Christian to muster up votes from the religious right. Historian Wilbur Edel, for example, belittles Reagan's moral underpinnings by comparing him to fundamentalist televangelists Jim Bakker and Oral Roberts. "Reagan," remarked Edel, "blended the talents of an actor with those of a fundamentalist preacher." In his sardonic biography, *Sleepwalking Through History: America in the Reagan Years*, Haynes Johnson concurred with Edel's view. Of televangelists and Reagan, Haynes writes with sarcasm, "His message reflected theirs, or theirs his."

It's a shame the elite neglects this part of Reagan, because they forget that Reagan's moral compass helped redirect religion in world culture. He truly was a leader, not only on the political stage, but in the arena of world religion as well. He helped shape the morality, and thereby the actions, of millions of people in his own time and afterward. "Atheism is not an incidental element of communism, not just part of the package; it is the package," insisted Reagan in 1985. What the pundits saw as bankrupt political rhetoric soon became the source of a rich spiritual renewal worldwide. Religion would be reborn for hundreds of millions of people behind the Iron Curtain. Reagan's words, although not the only cause of communism's demise, certainly were one of the main factors that wrought worldwide religious freedom.

Before Reagan was leader of the "free world," communism prohibited more than a third of the world's population from practicing their faith. The religious—Christians, Jews, and Muslims—were imprisoned and murdered for their beliefs.

Churches were banned, public worship forbidden, and Bibles burned. For Reagan, communism was more than an economic and political calamity, but a spiritual crisis. "They [the Soviets] are the focus of evil in the modern world," argued Reagan. He said that we ought to "pray for the salvation of all those who live in totalitarian darkness" so that "they will discover the joy of knowing God." America was, in Reagan's view, a vital link in protecting biblical lineages going back to Genesis. "You," he told West Point cadets in 1981, "are a chain holding back an evil force that would extinguish the light we've been tending for 6,000 years."

Reagan lived to see the end of the dark age of religious repression in Eastern Europe and throughout the Soviet Union, where Protestant and Catholic churches now flourish, and where Jews, Pentecostals, and others who had been persecuted for their belief in God are now free to emigrate to Israel or other safer regions of the world. Since the end of World War II, these peoples had lived under an official atheism, where there was no God but the state. Today, they are free to worship as they please.

Reagan's insistence on religious liberty is certainly his most memorable moral achievement, an unmistakable example of how his spirituality affected the world. How Reagan viewed his God and country also affected other issues, both domestic and international. Abortions, for example, although not yet outlawed, became harder to come by and even today are still on the decline.

But even if the religious freedom of millions of souls had been the *only* effect of Reagan's moral compass, it's still somewhat remarkable that historians shrink from any substantive discussion of Reagan's spiritual language. While Lincoln, who possessed a deeply held moral and religious character and who relied on Scripture to propagate the cause of freedom in America, is honored for his spirituality, Reagan is either unnoticed or vilified for it. If such a man—a man sometimes credited with "winning" the cold war—so wholeheartedly embraced Christianity and gave credit to the Christian God for his triumph, perhaps we ought to take a second look.

That's why I aspired to compile this book—to help straighten the record. The addresses and writings, or portions thereof, in this book are intended to demonstrate this: Ronald Reagan offered America, and the world, a clearly defined Judeo-Christian worldview, in context of the American democratic political system, that profoundly influenced the course of human history. This book also demonstrates that although political expediency sometimes entered into the mix of how and what Reagan said about his God and country, the record demonstrates that he never abandoned his core beliefs and values. This can be said about few public officials today.

This book is the first to look at the moral and spiritual precepts of Ronald Reagan's public words and writings. It's not a thorough analysis of the subject, but it is a thorough presentation, because it includes portions of every meaningful address Reagan gave in his public life about God, religion, and morality. Because he devoted so much attention to religious themes, I believe history warrants that it all be captured in a single compendium for future students, historians, and political scientists to ponder. "We cannot escape history," said Lincoln. My purpose in compiling this book is to help prevent history from evading the truth about Ronald Reagan's God and country.

Studying the ideas and beliefs of modern politicians can be a tedious process because they seldom write anything more than speeches or letters. Unlike Jefferson or Hamilton, who wrote books about their beliefs, today's popular leaders tend to make short quips, rather than give long explanations of their ideological views. So even the more trivial comments, notes and letters, and extemporaneous remarks are important to document. When my publisher authorized me to do this work, I set my course on researching thousands of public documents, going back as far as 1961, in search of the substance of Reagan's spiritually laden rhetoric.

My own political persuasions are, admittedly, conservative. When I met Reagan—well, not the man himself, but the man I came to believe in through his words—I was just forming my ideologies. A latecomer to the Reagan revolution, I got my start in the political arena by managing congressional campaigns and working for the House of Representatives staff during the Bush administration. But, despite my conservative tendencies, I don't intend to promote my views, but only to offer the interested reader a unique anthology. To conservatives, and other supporters of President Reagan, this book should prove to be delightful reading. It's "the Great Communicator" at his best. For readers on the other side of the political spectrum, even if you ardently disagree with the contents of this book, you can't help but find them inspirational. Early in his presidency, Reagan commented that what he really wanted to do was to "go down in history as the president who made America believe in itself again." So maybe even the most disparaging critic might find reason to explore how and why Reagan's spiritual visions captivated America.

You'll find this book divided into eleven chapters, each encompassing a particular moral or religious focus of Reagan during his political career. Themes include spiritual renewal and revival, the sanctity of life, restoration of the family, prayer and national purpose, the Bible and culture, freedom from tyranny, hope for the future, the triumph of good over evil, patriotism in a democratic society, the conscience of a nation, and the Man from Galilee.

Most of the words in this book are Reagan's, and I've excerpted from them the essence of what he said or wrote about the subject matter. If I included everything Reagan said about God, my publisher probably couldn't afford to print this book, because there's simply so much material. I've kept my comments to a minimum. You'll find them only when they're necessary for background or clarification. Reagan never outlined in writing his religious approach to democracy and public service. Nevertheless, his words and practices follow identifiable patterns. I've tried to organize this book in such a way that the reader can identify these patterns.

This book would not have been possible without access to material compiled and published by the Office of the Federal Register, National Archives and Records Service, and General Services Administration, in the *Public Papers of the Presidents of the United States,* January 20, 1981–January 20, 1989. I would also like to express my gratitude to my editor, Bert Ghezzi, for the craft of his red pen and, most of all, for his moral support and friendship. Finally, I thank my sons, Nicholas and Matthew, for their patience and help as I scoured documents and prepared the contents of this book.

INTRODUCTION

WHAT DID REAGAN BELIEVE ABOUT GOD AND COUNTRY?

These days, it's hard to know what our elected officials believe about morality and religion. We hear a lot of stump speeches about faith and integrity, even about God, but the shifting sands of political expediency make it all but impossible to put your finger on what convictions, if any, our candidates hold true.

Ronald Reagan was no such man. His God was easy to recognize. Reagan's spiritual oratory was uncomplicated and astonishingly repetitive, partly because Reagan's theology didn't evolve much over the course of his life. Unlike Lincoln who, although religious, couldn't ever make up his mind about which religion to believe in, Reagan's core religious beliefs were always steeped in traditional Judeo-Christian heritage. Reagan's spiritual values were unencumbered by trendy spiritual whims, by the disparagements of his critics, and even by the personal tragedy and crisis that he suffered throughout his life. The convictions he was taught as a child were the same he held as an adult. The moral precepts he espoused early in his political career went unchanged nearly half a century later when he was elected president.

What Reagan believed and said about God concurred with the teachings of his devout mother, Nelle, and the Dixon Christian Church in which he was raised. The Christian Church, also known as the Disciples of Christ, taught that the

Bible contained all the truths necessary for a happy and moral life. It preached a simple, optimistic gospel, emphasizing the work ethic, equal rights, and individual responsibility. The Christian Church was not prone to much introspection. Although prayer and reading the Bible were important aspects of the Christian life, it was more important to be busy *doing* God's work, rather than *reflecting* on it. Success came only to those who were hardworking and disciplined. Disciples in the Dixon Christian Church believed in progress and reform— they were among the strongest supporters of the temperance and abolitionist movements in the nineteenth century—but were also highly suspicious of governmental intrusion in their daily lives.

Reagan's religious rhetoric borrowed heavily from the tenets of the Dixon Christian Church. His enduring optimism, support for working families, belief in individual freedom and responsibility, vigor for social reform, and, of course, his opposition to an intruding federal government, all were mirrored in the lessons he learned as a boy.

But even more fundamental to the Disciples of Christ doctrine and to Nelle was the strong belief in predestination or Divine Providence. More than any other precept Reagan learned as a youth, this one seemed to have impressed him the most.

Alexander Campbell, the nineteenth century religious frontiersman who co-founded the Disciples of Christ, popularized the idea that the American people were chosen by God to fulfill a special mission on earth. God was active in directing the affairs of history, taught Campbell, and every Christian citizen was predestined for a specific task in order to uphold the Republic and to spread the Gospel. God had blessed America with freedom and prosperity starting with the Pilgrims, and Americans—particularly Christian Americans—were expected to do their part by God's will to spread and protect that blessing abroad.

Of course, the belief that God had singled out America was not unique to Nelle Reagan and her church. Up until about halfway through the twentieth century, popular opinion swayed heavily on the side of Christian patriotism. But by later in the twentieth century "Pilgrim-style" Divine Providence had become an old-fashioned value. Modern historians and political observers dismissed the "myth of American uniqueness." For Reagan, though, who never lost touch with the values he learned as a child, Divine Providence was still a part of his worldview. In his political repertoire, it didn't go out of style.

Reagan believed, simply and unashamedly, that America had deserted the moral roots upon which it was founded, and that America's progress toward its God-given destiny had been deterred. As a result of breaking its moral covenant with God, America was plagued by a host of societal and economic problems: the breakdown of the family and community, the spread of atheism and communism, immorality and legalized abortion, an expanding federal government, a disintegrating economy, secularism in education, eroding patriotism, and a dwindling national defense. Not prone to pessimism, however, Reagan believed that through repentance and reformation, America would be revived once again and ultimately find its "rendezvous with destiny."

"We shall be a city on a hill," Reagan said over and over again as president. Reagan borrowed the "city on a hill message" from the Pilgrim John Winthrop, who left British despots in search of religious liberty and the pursuit of happiness. In 1630 he proclaimed from the deck of the Arabella, off the coast of Massachusetts, "We shall be a city on a hill. The eyes of all people are upon us so that if we shall deal falsely with our God in this work we have undertaken and so cause Him to withdraw His present help from us, we shall be made a story and a byword throughout the world." Reagan often evoked the prophetic-like words of Winthrop. With vigor and conviction, he recited the message that God predestined America for a unique purpose. He relentlessly pursued his efforts to set America back on the path for which God created it. And he cast himself as a modern-day Winthrop, inviting Americans to join him in a great national crusade to "recapture our destiny." "For I believe," said Reagan, "that Americans ... are every bit as committed to that vision of a shining city on a hill as were those long-ago settlers."

Reagan's belief in Divine Providence overshadowed everything else he believed about God and his country. Most of his spiritual oratory was derived from adapting this and other similar Puritan sermons into contemporary political rhetoric. In *Ronald Reagan: The Great Communicator*, authors Ritter and Henry explain how Reagan deftly recast some centuries-old religious sentiments.

> His [Reagan's] campaign argument was straightforward and hopeful: America had been blessed by God as the home of liberty. The constitutional concepts of individual freedom and limited governmental powers constituted America's covenant. Under it, America had flourished, ultimately becoming the most favored and most powerful nation in the world. But something had gone wrong. The people had

been misguided by leaders who violated the covenant, and the nation was suffering. The solution was to restore the original covenant and recover its blessings before it was too late. Reagan's message was a secular version of the religious jeremiads from the Old Testament prophets: "In every generation, sin leads to national disaster, but repentance to new life and salvation."

An Old Testament verse—2 Chronicles 7:14—spurred Reagan's belief that America could regain its moral bearings. Nelle had ingrained this verse in his mind and spirit. "If my people, which are called by my name, shall humble themselves, and pray, and seek my face, and turn from their wicked ways; then I will hear from heaven, and will forgive their sin, and will heal their land." This verse summed up just about everything Reagan believed about God and his country. He held his Bible open to this verse when inaugurated as president, and he cited it more than any other throughout his career in public service.

Aside from Divine Providence, what else did Reagan believe about God, the Bible, and his country? Reagan believed in the very basic foundations of Judaism and Christianity. He believed in the God of Abraham and Moses. He believed God had established the Ten Commandments as the moral foundation for future generations. He believed in the Bible as the inspired Word of God, and he interpreted it quite literally. Referring to the Bible, he once said, "... of the many influences that have shaped the United States of America into a distinctive nation and people, none may be said to be more fundamental and enduring than the Bible." America, according to Reagan, was founded on principles found in the Bible. "The Bible and its teachings helped form the basis for the Founding Fathers' abiding belief in the inalienable rights of the individual, rights which they found implicit in the Bible's teachings of the inherent worth and dignity of each individual," he once remarked. Democracy, then, was contingent upon belief in the Bible, not only as a historical document, but as the inspired Word of God given to man for guidance and reproof. He also believed one could look to the Bible for answers to life's problems. In fact, he believed that "inside its pages lie all the answers to all the problems that man has ever known."

He believed Jesus was more than a great moral teacher, but the actual incarnate Son of God. He believed in the power of prayer, that he could communicate with God and that God spoke to him through Scripture and through circumstances in his life. For Reagan, prayer was not to be paraded. It was personal, not a public display. Unlike other presidents, including President Bill Clinton, he never authorized himself to be photographed praying or reading the Bible. "Prayer, of course, is deeply personal," he said. "Many of us have been taught to pray by people we love. In my case, it was my mother. I learned quite literally at her knee. My mother gave me a great deal, but nothing she gave me was more important than that special gift, the knowledge of the happiness and solace to be gained by talking to the Lord."

Reagan believed that God created everyone equal and that all people should be free to worship God as they freely choose. He also believed it was incumbent upon America to secure the religious freedom of all people in the world. "I believe that the most essential element of our defense of freedom is our insistence on speaking out for the cause of religious liberty," he proclaimed. For Reagan, religious freedom was a human right worth fighting for. "I would like to see this country rededicate itself wholeheartedly to this cause ... We are our brothers' keepers, all of us ... Prisoners of conscience throughout the world, take heart; you have not been forgotten. We, your brothers and sisters in God, have made your cause our cause, and we vow never to relent until you have regained the freedom that is your birthright as a child of God." The right to freely worship God was inherent in each person. It was a birthright to be secured and protected.

He believed in the cosmic, eternal struggle of good versus evil. "Evil still stalks the planet," warned Reagan. Evil was a "government which was deliberately subverted by denouncing God, smothering faith, destroying freedom...." Evil was the Holocaust, "a grotesque effort to hurl the Earth into the very pit of the serpent." Evil was a government so "inherently unstable that it has no peaceful means to legitimize its leaders." Evil was communism, a "sad, bizarre chapter in human history whose last pages even now are being written." Why was communism so evil to Reagan? Because "the source of our strength in the quest for human freedom is not material, but spiritual."

Reagan believed that America had lost its spiritual roots, and that it was in desperate need of a spiritual revival. Reagan repeatedly remarked, "There is a spiritual hunger in this country today." It was a unique aside, coming from a politician, but it resonated with voters in a way not unlike words coming from a minister. Reagan was aware of how similar this appeal must have sometimes sounded to a preacher's sermons, admitting his role was "... a little bit like a minister." Still, it was Reagan's core belief since his early days in Dixon, Iowa, that America was losing her spiritual roots and was in need of a civic revival of religion and patriotism.

Reagan believed family values played a central role in

American history, and that they ought to continue to be central. Why were family values so important to Reagan? He explained the reasons for his beliefs in 1983: "Family life and the life of freedom are interdependent. In the arena of the family, children learn the most important lessons they will ever receive about their inherent dignity as individuals. They learn as well about the social and religious traditions that unite generation to generation, and they begin to acquire the values for which their ancestors sacrificed so much for freedom." To his credit, Reagan realized that times had changed. He didn't intend that the clock be turned back. "I'm not talking about nostalgia for the past," he said, "but refinding what worked about the past and bringing it into the present and the future. Refinding our bearings, forging a sense of continuity where it doesn't exist outwardly in the facts of our lives, we have to recreate connections—connections with our family, between the family and the community."

Reagan believed in the constitutional rights of unborn children. "The values and freedoms we cherish as Americans rest on our fundamental commitment to the sanctity of human life," wrote Reagan in 1984. Reagan opposed abortion, on the basis of the most basic, God-given rights. He wrote, "The first of the 'unalienable rights' affirmed by our Declaration of Independence is the right to life itself, a right the Declaration states has been endowed by our Creator on all human beings—whether young or old, weak or strong, healthy or handicapped." All of Reagan's appointments to the Supreme Court opposed the Court's 1972 decision in *Roe v. Wade*. Dinesh D'Souza points out that many of Reagan's aides "begged him to stay away from the subject." But Reagan refused, even allowing the controversial, anti-abortion film

The Silent Scream to be shown at the White House. It should be noted that the abortion issue is probably the only moral issue on which Reagan changed his mind. Early in his political career, Reagan signed into California law a liberal abortion measure. He immediately regretted his choice and for the next three decades stood his ground against the murder of innocent unborn children.

Reagan also believed primary and secondary education had gone awry, due to anti-God, secular influences, a lack of time-honored discipline, and especially the lack of prayer in public schools. "If we could get God and discipline back in our schools, maybe we could get drugs and violence out," stumped Reagan. "God, the source of all knowledge, should never have been expelled from our children's classrooms," he said. Since very early in his political career, as early as his first nationally televised speech in 1964, Reagan pushed hard for prayer in public schools. It's interesting to note that Reagan's school prayer platform was established long before evangelicals became an organized force in American politics. So for those who think Reagan created the issue to cater to the Christian right, it should be recognized that it wasn't evangelical Christians who first pressed the issue. It was Reagan.

Can We Take Reagan at His Word?

Reagan's detractors complained about his religious commentaries. "What bothers me is this growing tendency to try to use one's own personal interpretation of faith politically, to question others' faith, and to try to use the instrumentalities of government to impose those views on others," grumbled presidential candidate Walter Mondale in 1984. Reagan biographer Paul D. Erickson called Reagan's views on God's presence in American history a "cynical manipulation of subliminal history." To the liberal establishment, and to many in the media, Reagan's spiritual remarks were objectionable and offensive, but to their dismay, his expressions of faith had become enormously popular with the public. As the editorial exasperation in the nation's newspapers heightened, one bewildered reporter quizzed Reagan, "I wonder, do you think it's appropriate to use the Bible in defending a political argument?" Although the question was asked with some disdain, this critique, and others, are worth examining.

The criticism against Reagan's religious rhetoric generally went as follows:

- Reagan's religious commentary was only meant to woo conservative Protestant voters. It was political posturing, pure and simple.

- Reagan's views on God and country weren't personal, but only public rhetoric. For someone who talked so much about God, he didn't attend church, or have a theology.

- Reagan's strong views on morality and religion were developed only after he was elected president. How can we believe an old man who has ignored religion for all of his adult life, and suddenly professes he's a Christian?

- Reagan was an actor whose religious rhetoric was written by speechwriters. He didn't originate the material, just marketed it effectively.

Let's face it, if we can't take Reagan for his own words, then there's not much sense in studying them, except for the sake of studying the manipulation of a democratic society. But, if we can acknowledge that Reagan was sincere in his beliefs, that his moral and spiritual underpinnings were more statesman-like and political, then this part of his legacy ought to be considered by future historians with the same deference afforded to Lincoln—even if you disagree with him. So, let's take a brief look at the common myths about Reagan's religious worldview.

Myth #1: Reagan's religious commentary was only meant to woo conservative Protestant voters. It was political posturing, pure and simple.

Unlike Reagan's colleagues in public service, who avoided speaking to religious institutions, Reagan purposefully sought to engage members of the clergy about the more existential meanings of American life. It's generally assumed, however, that Reagan engaged only evangelical Christian audiences, not other less fundamentalist groups. Author Haynes Johnson protested that Reagan "locked out" theological liberals and moderates. "No president during this century has so completely snubbed the established religious leadership of this nation as Ronald Reagan," he alleged.

Well, the Pope mustn't be a part of the religious establishment, then, because Reagan communicated with the Vatican more than any other American president has. Indeed, during my research, I found that contrary to popular misconceptions, Reagan's religious rhetoric was *not* devoted solely to conservative Protestantism. In fact, it was Reagan himself who flatly refused to describe himself as a "born-again" Christian in a 1984 debate with Walter Mondale. "I don't know whether I would fit that—that particular term [born-again]," said Reagan. For Reagan, the politically expedient answer would have been "yes." Evangelical Christians, who were growing in numbers and in organization, would have heartily approved and, after all, his predecessor, Jimmy Carter, set the precedent by describing himself as a born-again Christian. Yet Reagan didn't allow himself to be "coined" as such. He certainly endorsed many of the issues that were important to evangelicals, but never described himself as one and, as president, he addressed a much broader spectrum of religious groups, including Jewish and Catholic, than just fundamentalist Christian.

Why is it, then, the general public assumes Reagan endeared himself only to the Christian right wing? In part, it's because politicized, right-wing Christian organizations expressed such great public delight in the president's views, as juxtaposed to the media, who expressed such great public distress. In short, both the media of the Christian right and the mass media made much ado anytime Reagan spoke to or about issues that mattered to the Christian right. Hence, Reagan was publicly portrayed as a religious conservative. But the record shows that Reagan made about as many appeals to Catholic and Jewish groups as he did to Protestant ones, just with much less public attention.

For example, Reagan lavishly celebrated Jewish holidays with lengthy proclamations and special radio addresses, and went to great lengths to make mention of Jewish heritage in his annual Christmas proclamations. He paid special tribute to Jewish leaders, such as award-winning author Elie Wiesel. As president, he spoke regularly to Jewish organizations, including B'nai B'rith, the congregation of Temple Hillel, and the

U.S. Holocaust Memorial Council, about the horrors of the Holocaust. "It's incumbent upon us all, Jews and Gentile alike, to remember the tragedy of Nazi Germany," wrote Reagan in one of his many published papers directed to Jewish audiences (he published more papers to Jewish audiences than any previous president). The plight of Jews in the Soviet Union also troubled Reagan. "They are constantly ridiculed, harassed, beaten, and arrested by Soviet authorities," he told the Jewish Community Center, in Washington, D.C. "We must not forsake them. We will not be silent," he contended. When pressed once to answer questions about whether or not God hears the prayers of Jews, Reagan quickly retorted, "Since both the Christian and Judaic religions are based on the same God, the God of Moses, I'm quite sure those prayers are heard." Reagan's affinity for Judaism, and his support for Israel, seemed to be more than just political pragmatism, but spiritual as well. His belief in the Old Testament—the shared heritage of Jew and Christian—appeared to be, at least in part, the origin of Reagan's pro-Semitic stance.

Addressing the congregation at Temple Hillel, he suggested, "All of us here are descendents of Abraham, Isaac, and Jacob, sons and daughters of the same God." Reagan made similar statements about Judaism throughout his public life, and in 1982 when he sent American soldiers to Lebanon, to protect Israel, he reportedly was identifying with Ezekiel's great-winged eagle: A great eagle with large wings and long pinions, full of feathers of various colors, came to Lebanon and took from the cedar the highest branch (see Ez 17:3).

Reagan also spoke regularly to Catholic organizations, more so than any other previous American president. He addressed the New York Federation of Catholic Schools, the National

Catholic Education Association, Georgetown University, Catholic Irish groups, and he appeared in three separate ceremonies with Pope John Paul II. He worked with the Vatican to bolster Catholic churches in Poland, and to the chagrin of some evangelicals, Reagan opened full-fledged, official diplomatic relations with the Vatican. It was then that he proclaimed "the consequence of our efforts deserves nothing less, for we join with the Holy See in our concern for a world of peace, where armaments are reduced and human rights respected, a world of justice and hope, where each of God's creatures has the means and opportunity to develop to his or her full potential." Not even John F. Kennedy, the first Catholic president, was willing to make so many direct appeals to a pope as did Reagan.

Near the end of Reagan's tenure in office, he offered a vigorous defense of the Christian faith, relying on the teachings of St. Thomas Aquinas, to a group of Catholic students:

I have come here today as a temporal leader, a man concerned with the affairs of state, and the course of the country. And yet I have come to tell you, my young friends, in all my years of public life, I have found that what [Saint Thomas] Aquinas tells us is necessary for the happiness of man is also necessary for the strength and happiness of nations ... So this is my message to you, as a secular leader, but also as a man standing in humility before God: to seek what the Cardinal [Hickey] calls true freedom, to reach for what Aquinas called the necessities of salvation. For if you do, if these lessons become part of the instruction you carry with you when you end your studies here, America will be stronger; the world will be better; and there will be no limits to what, in this sweet land of liberty, you can do with your lives.

Although Reagan's apologetic was always ecumenical, it was admittedly in front of evangelical Christian audiences that he seemed to feel most at home. For the term of his presidency, he addressed the annual conventions of both the National Association of Evangelicals (NAE) and the National Religious Broadcasters (NRB). Both groups represented the growing, and organized, constituencies of evangelical Christian churches, ministries, and missions organizations. Among the leaders of NAE and NRB were nationally-recognized Christian media personalities including Pat Robertson and Jerry Fallwell. On no less than a dozen occasions, President Reagan gave lengthy speeches to these organizations. One speech, given on March 8, 1983, to the NAE, was probably the single most important speech of his presidency. It was in this address he first described the Soviet Union as the "evil empire." "There is sin and evil in the world," proclaimed Reagan, "and we are enjoined by Scripture and the Lord Jesus to oppose it with all our might."

When he spoke to evangelical Christians, both the words he used and his tone of delivery were heightened. It is when he addressed these audiences that he made his strongest case for prayer in the public schools and outlawing abortion. It's also when he made his most personal remarks about the truth of Christianity, the power of prayer, and even what Christ had meant in his own life. "His name alone, Jesus, can lift our hearts, soothe our sorrows, heal our wounds, and drive away our fears. He gave us love and forgiveness. He taught us truth and left us hope," said a passionate Reagan to the NRB in 1983.

But the notion that he catered only to conservative Protestants is simply unfounded by the record. Reagan himself once adeptly explained his position when a reporter chided the President for promoting "... Christ as coming from a president who is a man in a nonsectarian office." Reagan replied:

You may recall that at the lighting of the Christmas tree that I said that on that birthday of the man from Galilee, there are those in our land who recognized him as a prophet or a great teacher, or a man and just a teacher. And there are those who believe that he was of divine origin and the Son of God. And whichever, we celebrated his birthday with respect to the man.

Reagan was careful then, and throughout his presidency, to align himself to the moral causes that were important to him, not just to any particular denomination or belief. He professed Christian beliefs, and recognized the vital role of the Christian faith in American history, yet never used his official capacity to propagate belief in the Christian gospel.

Myth #2: Reagan's views on God and country weren't personal, but only public rhetoric. For someone who talked so much about God, he didn't attend church, or possess a theology.

Another reason critics might have thought Reagan to be disingenuous in his religious rhetoric was his own approach to church attendance. Despite the fact that Reagan said so much in public about spirituality he, admittedly, held organized religion at arm's length. Like Lincoln, he didn't attend church regularly—at least not as president, nor did he identify himself with any particular Christian denomination.

Edel also suggests that Reagan was insincere because of the "absence of any but passing reference to religion in his memoirs." It is somewhat notable that Reagan doesn't mention more about his religious upbringing in his own memoirs, *An American Life,* because, according to journalist George Will, Reagan was "as close to being a minister's kid as one can be without actually moving into the rectory."

The fact, though, is that Reagan did have a strong sense of communion with the divine. He claimed to have been miraculously healed of a stomach ulcer in the late 1960s, to have once heard the audible voice of his deceased father, and to have received a "prophecy" that he would become president—ten years before he was elected. "No, it isn't easy for me to talk about this," admitted Reagan when questioned about his personal religious views and experiences. Apparently, it wasn't easy for him to write about it either. But his upbringing certainly brings to mind his closeness to Christianity.

Reagan's mother, Nelle, was a devout Christian, and raised young Reagan according to the strict teachings of the Christian Church. Television producer Adrinana Bosch, who researched Reagan's childhood for the PBS television series, *The American Experience,* said Reagan "imbibed deeply from his mother's faith." It was what caused those closest to him to "attest to his spirituality, and his strong belief in predestination and the power of prayer." Anne Edwards, in her voluminous book, *Early Reagan,* interviewed neighbors, and members of Dixon Christian church, where the Reagans attended, to show what an integral part faith played in young Reagan's life. As a grammar student, Reagan led Sunday school classes, Bible studies, and prayer sessions. Parishioners recounted how Reagan "made the Bible seem personal, like a phrase might just have been written." He attended church several times a week, for many years, and was recognized in his community as a moral, upstanding young person. Reagan's choice of college, Eureka College, itself founded by the Christian Church, has a reputation for being "old-timey ... a Bible school after all." The Eureka 1936 student handbook read, "Religious values shall be found in all courses of study, in the work plan, and in recreational activities. The development of religious attitudes ... is essential." Edwards says, "there the Bible was a daily and vital part of his [Reagan's] life."

Faith, however, didn't seem to play a role in Reagan's Hollywood ventures, where there's virtually no evidence at all that he prayed, worshipped, or practiced religion. He didn't lead an immoral life in Hollywood. On the contrary, he rarely drank, didn't smoke or gamble, and refused to carouse with his Hollywood colleagues. He was "never for the sexpots. He was never looking for the bed," said an old friend. It wasn't until he was elected governor that he returned to the faith of his childhood. "He had not mentioned religion very often during his halcyon days when he was riding high in Hollywood. But as he became more mature and had to wrestle with the responsibilities of high office, he acquired a new appreciation of the time and effort his mother spent in teaching him the need for daily prayer," wrote journalist Frank van der Linden. Reagan told van der Linden that it was then, as governor, that he spent more time in prayer "than in any previous period I can recall."

Even then, though, Reagan was not given much to introspection. His spirituality was simple and straightforward. "I think it is very plain that we are given a certain control of our destiny because we are given the chance to choose," said Reagan. "We are given a set of rules or guidelines in the Bible by which to live and it is up to us to decide whether we will abide by them or not."

Although Reagan did not attend church regularly as president, he had been a member of Bel Air Presbyterian Church, in California, where he would sometimes personally call the pastor, Rev. Donn D. Moomaw, after hearing a sermon. Moomaw's recollections were that Reagan was "very intelligent in his knowledge of the Scriptures," but also that Reagan once "readily admitted difficulty in being vocal about his faith." Some of Reagan's closest friends, though, found Reagan to be very interested in Christianity. One friend and advisor, Michael Deaver, said that "Ronald Reagan is nuts for religious phenomena.... He reads whatever he can get his hands on, watches any movie or television show that deals with the subject." Another Reagan confidant, Frank van der Linden, once wrote, "Despite his many years before the public, Reagan has remained essentially a mystery to many of his fellow Americans; and they are surprised to discover that he is deeply religious."

Dinesh D'Souza, former senior domestic policy analyst in the Reagan White House, noted that aides closest to President Reagan would occasionally see him get down on his knees and pray, and was sometimes visibly moved and wept when prayed for by visiting pastors. D'Souza notes that Reagan's "private beliefs can best be gauged from his personal correspondence in a letter Reagan personally penned in 1978." The letter was in response to one delivered to Reagan, from a minister. The minister disavowed belief that Christ was the Son of God. Reagan replied,

Christ's own statements foreclose, in my opinion, any questions as to his divinity. It doesn't seem to me that he gave us any choice: either he was what he said he was, or he was the world's greatest liar. It is impossible for me to believe that a liar or charlatan could have had the effect on mankind that he has for 2,000 years. We would ask: would even the greatest of liars carry his lie through the Crucifixion when a simple confession would have saved him?

Reagan also gave us a glimpse of his own personal theology in one of his presidential diaries. When Reagan learned that his wife's father was on his deathbed, his entry that night was short, and said simply, "I want so much to speak to him about faith. He's always been an agnostic; now I think he knows fear for probably the first time in his life. I believe this is a moment when he should turn to God and I want so much to help him do that." His daughter, Maureen, said, "He always believed that whatever happens, it's for a reason, and he has always been able to reach down inside and pull out a belief in a Supreme Being that has been able to get him through his roughest times."

What about the church issue? Reagan's lack of interest in going to church, as president, caused skepticism during the tenure of his term in office. Former attorney general Edwin Meese III addressed the issue reflectively in 1998:

He [Reagan] had a very strong personal faith, which came up as a natural thing in private conversation. The president was able to talk about religion in a comfortable way, better than almost any person I've ever met. He did not want to parade it before the public, where people would think he was using it for political purposes or to try to engender the idea that he was a religious man.... He felt that if he went out to a regular church service, he would disrupt it. As soon as he left the presidency, he became a regular churchgoer.

Not only did Reagan not like to be seen in churches, he refused to be photographed praying or reading a Bible. Despite Reagan's public professions of faith, in a public context, he was reticent to display his own personal beliefs for public grandeur.

Myth #3: Reagan's strong views on morality and religion were developed only after he was elected president. How can we believe an old man who has ignored religion for all of his adult life, and suddenly professes he's a Christian?

During a press conference in 1984, a reporter who had listened to President Reagan's spirited NRB speech suggested that he was somehow fallaciously "preaching the Gospel of Christ." "It just doesn't seem like you in the past," reasoned the reporter. Reagan didn't defend the nature of his speech, but responded simply, "Maybe others haven't listened to me in the past."

Apparently, many hadn't listened closely. The truth is that Reagan had been talking about religion for more than forty years. He brought God into his political portfolio long before he expressed any interest in running for national office. By his own admission, Reagan had always called himself a "mystic." "I've always believed that we were—each of us—put here for a reason," wrote Reagan, "that there is a plan, a divine plan for all of us. In an effort to embrace that plan, we are blessed with the special gift of prayer, the happiness and solace to be gained by talking to the Lord."

For almost four decades before he was elected president, Reagan was associating godliness with his public policy initiatives. Even before he was elected governor of California, he insisted at a Chamber of Commerce meeting, in 1961, that the American tax systems ought to resemble the Bible's teaching on tithing. "We are told we should give the Lord one-tenth, and if the Lord prosper us ten times as much, we should give ten times as much."

When elected governor of California, he suggested that churches take over the welfare system. In his inaugural address to the California State Assembly, he boldly quoted Benjamin Franklin: "He who introduces into public office the principles of primitive Christianity will change the face of the world." "It is inconceivable to me," he continued, "that anyone could accept this delegated authority without asking God's help, and I pray that we who legislate and administer will be granted wisdom and strength beyond our own limited power, that with Divine guidance we can avoid easy expedients ..." He told David Frost in 1968 that Jesus was the historical figure he admired the most, and later mentioned that he wanted to run the office of governor according to the teachings of Jesus. He proclaimed, "Belief in the dependence on God is essential to our state and nation. This will be an integral part of our state as long I have anything to do with it." He invited Billy Graham to address a joint session of the California State Legislature, and even went so far as to arrange a private meeting with Graham and his own gubernatorial cabinet about the second coming of Christ. "For the first time ever, everything is in place for the battle of Armageddon and the second coming of

Christ," said Reagan to a surprised audience at a banquet for California Senate president pro tem James Mills.

In his first nationally televised address in 1964, Reagan scolded the courts for judging that "a child's prayer in a school cafeteria endangers religious freedom." He concluded that speech with references to both Moses and Jesus. In 1967, in a commencement address at his alma mater, Eureka College, he asked the question, "Can you name one problem that would not be solved if we had simply followed the teachings of the man from Galilee?" In 1977, Reagan explained the cause of the Republican Party should be "to rediscover, reassert, and reapply America's spiritual heritage to our national affairs." By the time he ran for president, in 1980, he included some religious reference in almost every address or appeal.

So it goes, throughout his public life, Reagan pursued the subject of religion, well, religiously. It wasn't an after-effect of his being elected to high office, but an important part of his life and actions during every political campaign he waged. Certainly, when elected president, his public words were scrutinized on a much higher level than when he crisscrossed the country in the 1960s and 1970s, speaking in churches and to small civic organizations. But even so, his moral appeals didn't gain with him, but with the general public at large.

Myth #4: Reagan was an actor whose religious rhetoric was written by speechwriters from the Christian right wing. Reagan didn't originate the material, just marketed it effectively.

Other critics suggested that Reagan was more ambivalent about God than he might seem, that he might be sincere in his basic beliefs, yet the words he spoke weren't his own but those of his aides and speechwriters. He was just an actor—a professional cue-card reader—playing out words much like he did in Hollywood studios.

This is the most mythical of all the objections raised by Reagan's critics. If it were true, if Reagan had deferred all depth of meaning in his speeches to speechwriters, then reading this book wouldn't be any different from reading the script to *Knute Rockne: All American,* in which Reagan played the role of "the Gipper."

This misconception was sparked early on in Reagan's political career by Pat Brown, who ran against Reagan in the 1964 California gubernatorial campaign. Brown characterized Reagan as "only an actor who memorizes speeches written by other people, just like he memorized the lines that were fed to him by his screenwriters in the movies." The record, though, is to the contrary. A perturbed Reagan privately responded to Pat Brown's accusation, "Well, I *was* writing my own speeches. But I couldn't get up and say to an audience, 'Hey, I write my own speeches.'"

So Reagan routinely ignored all such accusations. But those closest to Reagan, those who worked with him on the campaign trails and in the White House, duly noted that he actively participated in writing and editing his own speeches.

Longtime aide Martin Anderson wrote, "He [Reagan] was a tremendous speechwriter. In the early days of the campaign, he wrote all of his speeches.... He liked to write on long yellow legal pads. He wrote in black ink." "He really marks them up ... new paragraphs, deletions, additions all over the place," remarked a White House speechwriter. Bently Elliot, Reagan's former director of speech writing, commented that "speech-writing is all the more important to this particular president [Reagan] because he is so gifted in being able to express his convictions." Elliot characterized Reagan's own speeches as "very concisely written," and said that he had "a tremendous austerity in style." William Ken Muir Jr., former speechwriter for President George Bush, said Reagan was a "master stylist," and that he was so consistent in his style and substance that "as speech writerreplaced speechwriter, the difference was hardly detectable." Another speechwriter commented,

> I've seen it a hundred times. Say we were flying back East to do a speech. We would put him in a seat and just forget about him. He would work with a felt-tip pen. From his briefcase he would take two cards out of the Cincinnati speech and one card out of the Cleveland speech and two from some other speech ... he would continue to work until he got to the hotel. He'd rest, take a shower, and work on the cards. He'd get into the elevator and work on the cards again. He'd go to a staging area and work on the cards some more. He wants to do well. He wants to be perfect.

It was, in fact, the index cards that led many to believe he was simply reading scripted material, when in fact it was Reagan himself who wrote the words. It was a practice he developed on the California campaign trail. Jim Gibson, who worked with Reagan during the 1966 campaign, remembered Reagan would, in the evening, stay in his hotel room writing on index cards instead of associating with his staff.

Reagan Forever

In 1976, upon hearing the news that he had lost the Republican presidential nomination to the incumbent president Gerald Ford, Reagan recited to a gathering of his supporters an old Scottish ballad: "Lay me down and bleed awhile, though I am wounded, I am not slain. I shall rise to fight again." Political observers probably snickered a bit. He was, after all, an older man, nearing the end of his life and career. But one lone supporter among the thousands of people there held high a placard, which read simply "Reagan Forever." Four years later, upon accepting his party's presidential nomination, he concluded his remarks with a gesture to both the country and God he loved, a moment of silent prayer. The silence probably deafened the ears of those who tried to stop Reagan's ascent to the Oval Office, but to those who agreed with Reagan's philosophies, it spoke loud and clear.

Although Reagan the man won't last forever, the words and prayers he offered to America, and to the world, will endure. They'll live in the hearts and minds of those he inspired and, most importantly, in the millions of souls behind the Iron Curtain who now worship God freely. For them, Reagan's God and country will always have eternal meaning.

1 | FREEDOM FROM TYRANNY

> You may jail your people. You may sieze their goods. You may ban their unions. You may bully their rabbis and dissidents. You may forbid the name of Jesus to pass their lips. But you will never destroy the love of God and freedom that burns in their hearts. They will triumph over you. –1983

Created to Be Free

The prophet Isaiah admonished the world, "Bind up the broken-hearted to proclaim liberty to the captives." Some twenty-five centuries later, philosophers would declare that "the cause of freedom is the cause of God."

We Americans understand the truth of these words. We were born a nation under God, sought out by people who trusted in Him to work His will in their daily lives, so America would be a land of fairness, morality, justice, and compassion.

Many governments oppress their people and abuse human rights. We must oppose this injustice. But only one so-called revolution puts itself above God, insists on total control over the people's lives, and is driven by the desire to seize more and more lands. As we mark this twenty-fifth observance of Captive

Nations Week, I have one question for those rulers: If communism is the wave of the future, why do you still need walls to keep people in and armies of secret police to keep them quiet?

Democracy may not be perfect, but the brave people who risk death for freedom are not fleeing from democracy—they're fleeing to democracy from communism.

Two visions of the world remain locked in dispute. The first believes all men are created equal by a loving God who has blessed us with freedom. Abraham Lincoln spoke for us: "No man," he said, "is good enough to govern another without the other's consent."

The second vision believes that religion is opium for the masses. It believes that eternal principles like truth, liberty, and democracy have no meaning beyond the whim of the state. And Lenin spoke for them: "It is true, that liberty is precious," he said, "so precious that it must be rationed."

Well, I'll take Lincoln's version over Lenin's and so will citizens of the world if they're given free choice.... With faith as our guide, we can muster the wisdom and will to protect the deepest treasures of the human spirit—the freedom to build a better life in our time and the promise of life everlasting in His kingdom....

-Remarks at a ceremony marking the annual observance
of Captive Nations Week, July 19, 1983

The Responsibilities of Freedom

In the early days of our country, our first president, George Washington, visited a Hebrew congregation in Newport, Rhode

Island. In response to their address, he wrote them a now rather famous letter reflecting on the meaning of America's newly won freedom. He wrote, "All possess alike liberty of conscience and immunities of citizenship. For happily the government of the United States, which gives to bigotry no sanction, to persecution no assistance, requires only that they who live under its protection should demean themselves as good citizens."

Well, certainly our country doesn't have a spotless record, but our fundamental beliefs, the ones that inspired Washington when he penned that letter, are sound. Our whole way of life is based on a compact between good and decent people, a voluntary agreement to live here together in freedom, respecting the rights of others and expecting that our rights in return will be respected.

But the freedom we enjoy carries with it a tremendous responsibility. You, the survivors of the Holocaust, remind us of that. Good and decent people must not close their eyes to evil, must not ignore the suffering of the innocent, and must never remain silent and inactive in times of moral crisis....

For just as the genocide of the Holocaust debased civilization, the outcome of the struggle against those who ran the camps and committed the atrocities gives us hope that the brighter side of the human spirit will, in the end, triumph.

Earlier, I described our country as a compact between good and decent people. I believe this, because it is the love of freedom, not nationalistic rituals and symbols, that unites us. And because of this, we are also bound in spirit to all those who yearn to be free and to live without fear. We are the keepers of the flame of liberty.

I understand that in Hebrew, the word for "engraved" is

charut. It is very similar to the word for "freedom," *cheyrut*. Tonight, we recognize that for freedom to survive and prosper it must be engraved in our character, so that when confronted with fundamental choices we will do what is right—because that is our way.

Looking around this room tonight I realize that although we come from many lands, we share a wealth of common experiences. Many of us remember the time before the Second World War. How we and our friends reacted to certain events has not faded from our memory. There are also in this room many young people, sons and daughters, maybe even a few grand-children. Perhaps some of the younger ones can't understand why we're making so much of a fuss. Perhaps some of them think we're too absorbed by the heartaches of the past and should move on.

Well, what we do tonight is not for us; it's for them. We who are old enough to remember must make certain those who take our place understand. So, if a youngster should ask you why you're here, just tell that young person, "because I love God, because I love my country, because I love you...."

-Remarks to the American Gathering of Jewish
Holocaust Survivors, April 11, 1983

Religion Is the Cause of Freedom

The history of religion and its impact on civilization cannot be summarized in a few days, never mind minutes. But one of the great shared characteristics of all religions is the distinction they draw between the temporal world and the spiritual world. All religions, in effect, echo the words of the Gospel of St. Matthew: "Render, therefore, unto Caesar the things which are Caesar's; and unto God the things that are God's." What this injunction teaches us is that the individual cannot be entirely subordinate to the state, that there exists a whole other realm, an almost mysterious realm of individual thought and action which is sacred and which is totally beyond and outside of state control. This idea has been central to the development of human rights.

Only in an intellectual climate which distinguishes between the city of God and the city of man and which explicitly affirms the independence of God's realm and forbids any infringement by the state on its prerogatives, only in such a climate could the idea of individual human rights take root, grow, and eventually flourish.

We see this climate in all democracies and in our own political tradition. The founders of our republic rooted their democratic commitment in the belief that all men are endowed by their Creator with certain inalienable rights. And so, they created a system of government whose avowed purpose was and is the protection of those God-given rights.

But as all of you know only too well, there are many political regimes today that completely reject the notion that a man or a woman can have a greater loyalty to God than to the state. Marx's central insight when he was creating his political system was that religious belief would subvert his intentions. Under the communist system, the ruling party would claim for itself the attributes which religious faith ascribes to God alone, and the state would be final arbiter of youth—or truth, I should say, justice and morality. I guess saying youth there instead of truth was just a sort of a Freudian slip on my part.

Marx declared religion an enemy of the people, a drug, an opiate of the masses. And Lenin said: "Religion and communism are incompatible in theory as well as in practice.... We must fight religion."

All of this illustrates a truth that, I believe, must be understood. Atheism is not an incidental element of communism, not just part of the package; it is the package. In countries which have fallen under communist rule, it is often the church which forms the most powerful barrier against a completely totalitarian system. And so, totalitarian regimes always seek either to destroy the church or, when that is impossible, to subvert it.

In the Soviet Union the church was immediately attacked by the communist revolution. But the Soviets, bowing to Western squeamishness about the denial of liberties, often characterize their actions as merely defensive.

In 1945 Josef Stalin met with Harry Hopkins, who had been sent by Harry Truman to discuss various East-West problems. In the middle of a talk about politics, Stalin interjected the following: In 1917, he said, the Russian Communist Party had proclaimed the right of religious freedom as part of their political program. But, he said, the churches of Russia had declared the Soviet government anathema and had called on church members to resist the call of the Red Army. Now, what could we do, said Stalin, but declare war on the church? He assured Hopkins, however, that World War II had ended the church-state antagonism and now freedom of religion could be granted to the church. But that, as you know, never happened.

History has taught us that you can bulldoze a church, but you can't extinguish all that is good in every human heart. And so, in spite of the dangers involved, there are Christians and Jews and Muslims and others throughout the communist world who continue to practice their faith....

But we mustn't feel despair, because it's not appropriate to the times. We're living in a dramatic age. Throughout the world the machinery of the state is being used as never before against religious freedom. But at the same time, throughout the world new groups of believers keep springing up. Points of light flash out in the darkness, and God is honored once again.

Perhaps this is the greatest irony of the communist experiment. The very pressure they apply seems to create the force, friction, and heat that allow deep belief to once again burst into flame.

I believe that the most essential element of our defense of freedom is our insistence on speaking out for the cause of religious liberty. I would like to see this country rededicate itself wholeheartedly to this cause. I join you in your desire that the Protestant churches of America, the Catholic Church, and the Jewish organizations remember the members of their flock who are in prison or in jeopardy in other countries. We are our brothers' keepers, all of us. And I hope the message will go forth: To prisoners of conscience throughout the world, take heart; you have not been forgotten. We, your brothers and sisters in God, have made your cause our cause, and we vow never to relent until you have regained the freedom that is your birthright as a child of God....

-Remarks at a conference on religious liberty,
April 16, 1985

The Right to Honor God

The most fitting way to mark the millennium of Christianity in Kiev Rus would be granting the right of all the peoples and all the creeds of the Soviet Union to worship their God, in their own way.

You have, of course, been hearing this afternoon about the first signs of progress. Some Soviet dissidents have been allowed to emigrate. Some churches have been allowed to organize and file for recognition, and recently the Soviets have said they will allow a printing of language Bibles. These are encouraging signs, and we welcome them. What we hope for ultimately is a willingness to see continued change in the spirit of *glasnost,* when it comes to matters of religion. Perhaps the process is beginning. We noted that General Secretary Gorbachev said recently, and I'll quote: "Mistakes made with regard to the church and believers in the 1930s and the years that followed are being rectified." Well, we sincerely hope and pray that this will be the case.

While some new churches are being built and others, mostly Russian Orthodox, have been allowed to reopen, many other congregations are denied recognition and, therefore, legality. The Ukrainian Catholic Church, the Uniate Church, is still closed, outlawed, and persecuted. Religious instruction of children outside the home—Sunday schools, Hebrew schools, or even confirmation classes—and the production of religious study material are all still illegal activities. And about those Bibles, the authorities have promised to print 100,000 copies for a country of 280 million people. Yet now, there are at least signs by Soviet authorities of a new law on the freedom of conscience, reflecting the interests of religious organizations.

So, while every positive step taken by the Soviets is welcomed, we realize that this is just a beginning. Let me also say, in particular, that the rights of Soviet Jews have taken up much of our official time, and this is very close to my heart. Our hope is for the doors to open fully to emigration and to full freedom for all faiths.

So, the earlier predictions by some that once the grandmothers died nobody would remember that there had been a church in Russia are wrong. Instead, the church in Russia is still full of grandmothers, women who were little children in 1917, and they're joined by the younger generation, longing to satisfy the need, the hunger, that no man-made institution in any society can ever fulfill. Today roughly 90 million people in the Soviet Union, or nearly a third of the population, proclaim some form of belief in God.

And it is not surprising that revolutions devoted to reshaping man as if he were so much clay deny one of the most basic teachings of Judeo-Christian belief: that after God shaped Adam from dust, he breathed into him the divine principle of life. There's a wonderful passage in *Doctor Zhivago*, in which Pasternak speaks of his bitter disillusionment with the philosophy of materialism and the bloody revolution it has spawned. "When I hear people speak of reshaping life," he says,

> I fall into despair. People who can say that have never understood a thing about life—they have never felt its breath, its heartbeat. They look on it as a lump of raw material that needs to be processed by them, to be ennobled by their touch. But life is never a material, a substance to be molded.

Life is the principle of self-renewal, it is constantly renewing
and remaking and changing and transfiguring itself, it is infinitely beyond your or my obtuse theories about it.

The history of the twentieth century has too often been
brutal and tragic, but it has taught us one lesson that should
fill our hearts with hope and joy, for we have found that the
more religion is oppressed, the greater the attempt to extinguish that life principle, that divine spark—the more it glows.
History is etched with stories of those who suffered religious
persecution, yes, but it also tells of transcendence, devotion,
and sanctity, even conversion.

We think of the strengthened conviction Aleksandr
Solzhenitsyn gained in prison, and the case of the Soviet psy-
chiatrist Anatoliy Koryagin, recently released after serving six
years in prison. He sought baptism as soon as he emigrated.
And we think of heroism and courage that can only remind us
of the early Christian martyrs. One such is Anna Chertkova,
recently released after being held in a Soviet psychiatric hospital since 1973 for no other crime than her faith; or Alfonsas
Svarinskas, a sixty-two-year-old Lithuanian priest, who has
spent eighteen years in prison and is not scheduled to be
released until 1990. He is gravely ill and has petitioned for
permission to go abroad to receive medical care; or Bishop
Julijonas Steponavicius, in internal exile since 1961 for refus-
ing to collaborate with the authorities.

How many men and women have had their faith tested?
Now we see some people, who have served prison sentences
for the unauthorized practice of religion, being released. And
no one has been imprisoned on that ground for the last two

years. Our hopes and prayers are for this expression of change by the Soviet authorities to continue.

The faith of the peoples of the Soviet Union is pure and unbreakable. As Moses led his people from bondage in Egypt, as the early Christians not only withstood pagan Rome but converted an empire, we pray that the millennium of Christianity in Kiev Rus will mean freedom for the faithful in Russia, in the Ukraine, the Baltic States, and all the regions of the Soviet Union. And if we pray, we might want to use the words of the 22nd Psalm: "In Thee our fathers trusted; they trusted, and Thou didst deliver them. To Thee they cried out and were delivered; in Thee they trusted and were not disappointed."

-Remarks at a White House briefing on religious
freedom in the Soviet Union, May 3, 1988

The Hope of Human Freedom

The hope of human freedom—the quest for it, the achievement of it—is the American saga. And I've often recalled one group of early settlers making a treacherous crossing of the Atlantic on a small ship when their leader, a minister, noted that perhaps their venture would fail and they would become a byword, a footnote to history. But, perhaps, too, with God's help, they might also found a new world, a city upon a hill, a light unto the nations. Those words and that destiny beckon to us still. Whether we seek it or not, whether we like it or not, we Americans are keepers of the miracles. We are asked to be guardians of a place to come to, a place to start again, a place to

live in the dignity God meant for his children. May it ever be so.
- Final radio address to the nation, January 14, 1989

Freedom's Extinction

In this land occurred the only true revolution in man's history. All other revolutions simply exchanged one set of rulers for another. Here for the first time the Founding Fathers—that little band of men so advanced beyond their time that the world has never seen their like since—evolved a government based on the idea that you and I have the God-given right and ability within ourselves to determine our own destiny. Freedom is never more than one generation away from extinction. We didn't pass it on to our children in the bloodstream. It must be fought for, protected, and handed on for them to do the same, or one day we will spend our sunset years telling our children and our children's children what it was once like in the United States when men were free.

-Remarks at the annual meeting of the Phoenix
Chamber of Commerce, March 30, 1961

Created as God's Children

We're still Jefferson's children, still believers that freedom is the inalienable right of all God's children. It's so precious, yet freedom is not something that can be touched, heard, seen, or smelled. It surrounds us, and if it were not present, as accustomed to it as we are, we would be alarmed, overwhelmed by outrage, or perhaps struck by a sense of being smothered. The air we breathe is also invisible and taken for granted, yet if it is denied even for a few seconds, we realize instantly how much it means to us. Well, so too with freedom. Freedom is not created by government, nor is it a gift from those in political power. It is, in fact, secured more than anything else by those limitations ... that are placed on those in government.

- Remarks announcing America's Economic
Bill of Rights, July 3, 1987

2 | HOPE FOR THE FUTURE

> My optimism comes not just from my strong faith in God, but from my strong and enduring faith in man. – 1991

America the Great

There is, in America, a greatness and a tremendous heritage of idealism which is a reservoir of strength and goodness. It is ours if we will but tap it. And, because of this—because that greatness is there—there is need in America today for a reaffirmation of that goodness and a reformation of our greatness.

The dialogue and the deeds of the past few decades are not sufficient to the day in which we live. They cannot keep the promise of tomorrow. The encrusted bureaucracies and the ingrained procedures which have developed of late respond neither to the minority nor the majority. We've come to a turning point. We have a decision to make. Will we continue with yesterday's agenda and yesterday's failures, or will we reassert our ideals and our standards, will we reaffirm our faith, and renew our purpose?

-Remarks at the Conservative Political
Action Committee, March 20, 1981

The Foolishness of America in Decline

Contrary to some of the things you've heard, I'm the same man I was when I came to Washington. I believe the same things I believed when I came to Washington. And I think those beliefs have been vindicated by the success of the policies to which we held fast. But now—just at the moment when we're required by history to hold the line, to hold true to our principles, and to apply the lessons of our learning, our faith, and our freedom—some of our most distinguished and thoughtful people have taken a look at the world today and determined that America is in decline.

America in decline? Orwell once said that some ideas were so foolish only intellectuals could believe them. Well, this is perhaps the most foolish idea of the present day. We live in the most prosperous, the freest society the world has ever known; and yet they say we're in decline. We've had almost six years of uninterrupted economic recovery, and yet they say we're in decline.

They say we're in decline because they believe we're spread too thin around the globe, that our military commitments are too vast and too difficult, and that we suffer from a condition called overstretch. Overstretch? Well, consider these truths. In 1955 we spent around 11 percent of our gross national product on defense. In 1988, around 6 percent—not quite enough, in my view, but still substantial. Some overstretch! In 1955 we had more than three million Americans in uniform. Today we have about two million Americans in uniform. Some overstretch!

And despite what you've heard, let the commander in chief assure you of one thing: We have not been accumulating nuclear weapons. In fact, the number of weapons in our nuclear stockpile was maybe a third higher twenty years ago. Today our weaponry is leaner, more accurate, and better equipped to keep the peace by keeping us strong. Some over-stretch!

I was given the honor of manning the nation's helm these past eight years, so I think I speak with some authority when I tell you, ladies and gentlemen, that the United States of America is not in decline. No, America is still young, still full of promise, and ready to fulfill that promise. She has not reached her apex. It's sad to say, but the false prophets of decline have needlessly lost faith at a moment when they should be taking faith. They should be taking faith in the ideas that have led us here: faith in the determination of men to be free and faith in the destiny our Maker has written for us. And, yes, ladies and gentlemen, with all my heart I believe that this is the age of freedom.

-Remarks at Georgetown University's
Bicentennial Convocation, October 1, 1988

God's Divine Plan for America

You can call it mysticism if you want to, but I have always believed that there was some divine plan that placed this great continent between two oceans to be sought out by those who were possessed of an abiding love of freedom and a special kind of courage.

This was true of those who pioneered the great wilderness in the beginning of this country, as it is also true of those later immigrants who were willing to leave the land of their birth and come to a land where even the language was unknown to them. Call it chauvinistic, but our heritage does set us apart....

We cannot escape our destiny, nor should we try to do so. The leadership of the free world was thrust upon us two centuries ago in that little hall of Philadelphia. In the days following World War II, when the economic strength and power of America was all that stood between the world and the return to the Dark Ages, Pope Pius XII said, "The American people have a great genius for splendid and unselfish actions. Into the hands of America God has placed the destinies of an afflicted mankind." We are indeed, and we are today, the last best hope of man on earth.

-Remarks at the Conservative Political
Action Conference, January 25, 1974

The Gift of Hope

Six years ago we came to Washington at a time of great national uncertainty. The vigor and confidence so evident in our land today reflect more than luck. They are the outgrowth of ideas that stress freedom for the individual and respect for the humane and decent values of family, God, and neighborhood. We are giving our children the greatest gift that is within our power to give, the one we received from those who came before us: a strong, free, and opportunity-filled America. And I thank you for all that you have done and continue to do to make certain that we do just that.

-Remarks at the Conservative Political
Action Conference, February 20, 1987

Have Faith in God

You can play a special part in the future. You'll be its author: Take full advantage of the wonderful life that lies in store for you. Rejoice in your freedom, sample the full richness of the opportunities that lie before you. Help one another, trust in yourselves, and have faith in God, and you'll find more joy and happiness than you could imagine. And always remember that you are Americans, and it is your birthright to dream great dreams in this sweet and blessed land, truly the greatest, freest, strongest nation on Earth.

-Remarks at the University of Virginia,
Charlottesville, December 16, 1988

Hope in Spiritual Hunger

We've come to a moment in our history when party labels are unimportant. Philosophy is all-important. Little men with loud voices cry doom, saying little is good in America. They create fear and uncertainty among us. Millions of Americans, especially our own sons and daughters, are seeking a cause they can believe in. There is a hunger in this country today—a hunger for spiritual guidance. People yearn once again to be proud of their country and proud of themselves. And there's every reason why they should be proud. Some may have failed America, but America has never failed us, and there is so much to be proud of in this land.

- Remarks at the Convention of Southern GOP,
Atlanta, Georgia, December 7, 1973

America's Best Days Are Yet to Come

We the people: Starting the third century of a dream and standing up to some cynic who's been trying to tell us we're not going to get any better. Are we at the end? Well, I can't tell it any better than the real thing—a story recorded by James Madison from the final moments of the Constitutional Convention, September 17, 1787. As the last few members signed the document, Benjamin Franklin—the oldest delegate, at eighty-one years, and in frail health—looked over toward the chair where George Washington daily presided. At the back of his chair was painted a picture of a sun on the horizon. Well, I know if we were there, we could see those delegates sitting around Franklin—leaning in to listen more closely to him. And then Dr. Franklin began to share his deepest hopes and fears about the outcome of their efforts, and this is what he said: "I have often looked at that picture behind the president without being able to tell whether it was a rising sun or a setting sun. But now at length I have the happiness to know that it is a rising sun and not a setting sun." Well, you can bet it's rising, because, my fellow citizens, America isn't finished. Her best is yet to come.

- Address before a joint session of Congress on
the State of the Union, January 27, 1987

3 | THE TRIUMPH OF GOOD OVER EVIL

> There is sin and evil in the world. And we are enjoined by Scripture and the Lord Jesus to oppose it with all our might. – 1983

Man Without God

We've heard in our century far too much of the sounds of anguish from those who live under totalitarian rule. We've seen too many monuments made not out of marble or stone but out of barbed wire and terror. But from these terrible places have come survivors, witnesses to the triumph of the human spirit over the mystique of state power, prisoners whose spiritual values made them the rulers of their guards. With their survival, they brought us "the secret of the camps," a lesson for our time and for any age: Evil is powerless if the good are unafraid.

That's why the Marxist vision of man without God must eventually be seen as an empty and a false faith—the second-oldest in the world—first proclaimed in the garden of Eden with whispered words of temptation: "Ye shall be as gods." The crisis of the Western world, Whittaker Chambers reminded us, exists to the degree in which it is indifferent to God. "The Western World does not know it," he said about our struggle, "but it already possesses the answer to this problem—but only provided that its faith in God and the freedom He enjoins is as great as communism's faith in man."

This is the real task before us: to reassert our commitment as a nation to a law higher than our own, to renew our spiritual strength. Only by building a wall of such spiritual resolve can we, as a free people, hope to protect our own heritage and make it someday the birthright of all men.

-Remarks at the Conservative Political
Action Committee, March 20, 1981

The Focus of Evil in the World

A number of years ago, I heard a young father, a very prominent young man in the entertainment world, addressing a tremendous gathering in California. It was during the time of the cold war, and communism and our own way of life were very much on people's minds. And he was speaking to that subject. And suddenly, though, I heard him saying, "I love my little girls more than anything—" And I said to myself, "Oh, no, don't. You can't—don't say that." But I had underestimated him. He went on: "I would rather see my little girls die now, still believing in God, than have them grow up under communism and one day die no longer believing in God."

There were thousands of young people in that audience. They came to their feet with shouts of joy. They had instantly recognized the profound truth in what he had said, with regard to the physical and the soul and what was truly important.

Yes, let us pray for the salvation of all those who live in that totalitarian darkness—pray they will discover the joy of knowing

God. But until they do, let us be aware that while they preach the supremacy of the state, declare its omnipotence over individual man, and predict its eventual domination of all people on the Earth, they are the focus of evil in the modern world.

It was C.S. Lewis who, in his unforgettable *Screwtape Letters*, wrote, "The greatest evil is not done now in those sordid 'dens of crime' that Dickens loved to paint. It is not even done in concentration camps and labor camps. In those we see its final result. But it is conceived and ordered (moved, seconded, carried, and minuted) in clear, carpeted, warmed, and well-lighted offices, by quiet men with white collars and cut fingernails and smooth-shaven cheeks who do not need to raise their voice."

Well, because these "quiet men" do not "raise their voices," because they sometimes speak in soothing tones of brotherhood and peace, because, like other dictators before them, they're always making their "final territorial demand," some would have us accept them at their word and accommodate ourselves to their aggressive impulses. But if history teaches anything, it teaches that simpleminded appeasement or wishful thinking about our adversaries is folly. It means the betrayal of our past, the squandering of our freedom.

So, I urge you to speak out against those who would place the United States in a position of military and moral inferiority. You know, I've always believed that old Screwtape reserved his best efforts for those of you in the church. So, in your discussions of the nuclear freeze proposals, I urge you to beware the temptation of pride—the temptation of blithely declaring yourselves above it all and labeling both sides equally at fault, to ignore the facts of history and the aggressive impulses of an evil empire, to simply call the arms race a giant misunderstanding and thereby remove yourself from the struggle between right and wrong and good and evil.

I ask you to resist the attempts of those who would have you withhold your support for our efforts, this administration's efforts, to keep America strong and free, while we negotiate real and verifiable reductions in the world's nuclear arsenals and one day, with God's help, their total elimination.

While America's military strength is important, let me add here that I've always maintained that the struggle now going on for the world will never be decided by bombs or rockets, by armies or military might. The real crisis we face today is a spiritual one; at root, it is a test of moral will and faith.

Whittaker Chambers, the man whose own religious conversion made him a witness to one of the terrible traumas of our time, the Hiss-Chambers case, wrote that the crisis of the Western world exists to the degree in which the West is indifferent to God, the degree to which it collaborates in communism's attempt to make man stand alone without God. And then he said, for Marxism-Leninism is actually the second oldest faith, first proclaimed in the garden of Eden with the words of temptation, "Ye shall be as gods."

The Western world can answer this challenge, he wrote, "but only provided that its faith in God and the freedom He enjoins is as great as communism's faith in man."

I believe we shall rise to the challenge. I believe that communism is another sad, bizarre chapter in human history whose last pages even now are being written. I believe this because the source of our strength in the quest for human freedom is not material, but spiritual. And because it knows no limitation, it must terrify and ultimately triumph over those who would enslave their fellow man. For in the words of Isaiah: "He giveth power to the faint; and to them that have no might He increased might."

Yes, change your world. One of our Founding Fathers, Thomas Paine, said, "We have it within our power to begin the world over again." We can do it, doing together what no one church could do by itself.

-Remarks at the annual convention of
the National Association of Evangelicals,
Orlando, Florida, March 8, 1983

Evil Stalks the Planet

Let us be frank. Evil still stalks the planet. Its ideology may be nothing more than bloodlust; no program more complex than economic plunder or military aggrandizement. But it is evil all the same. And wherever there are forces that would destroy the human spirit and diminish human potential, they must be recognized and must be countered.

-Remarks at the Oxford Union Society,
Oxford, England, December 4, 1982

The Rule of Law Under God

We're approaching the end of a bloody century plagued by a terrible political invention—totalitarianism. Optimism comes less easily today, not because democracy is less vigorous, but because democracy's enemies have refined their instruments of repression. Yet optimism is in order because day by day democracy is proving itself to be a not-at-all fragile flower. From Stettin on the Baltic to Varna on the Black Sea, the regimes planted by totalitarianism have had more than thirty years to establish their legitimacy. But none—not one regime—has yet been able to risk free elections. Regimes planted by bayonets do not take root. Historians looking back at our time will note the consistent restraint and peaceful intentions of the West. They will note that it was the democracies who refused to use the threat of their nuclear monopoly in the forties and early fifties for territorial or imperial gain. Had that nuclear monopoly been in the hands of the communist world, the map of Europe—indeed, the world—would look very different today. And certainly they will note it was not the democracies that invaded Afghanistan or suppressed Polish Solidarity or used chemical and toxin warfare in Afghanistan and Southeast Asia.

If history teaches anything, it teaches self-delusion in the face of unpleasant facts is folly. We see around us today the marks of our terrible dilemma—predictions of doomsday, antinuclear demonstrations, an arms race in which the West must, for its own protection, be an unwilling participant. At the same time we see totalitarian forces in the world who seek subversion and conflict around the globe to further their barbarous assault on the human spirit. What, then, is our course? Must civilization perish in a hail of fiery atoms? Must freedom wither in a quiet, deadening accommodation with totalitarian evil?

We cannot ignore the fact that even without our encouragement there have been and will continue to be repeated explosions against repression and dictatorships. The Soviet Union itself is not immune to this reality. Any system is inherently unstable that has no peaceful means to legitimize its leaders. In such cases, the very repressiveness of the state ultimately drives people to resist it, if necessary, by force.

While we must be cautious about forcing the pace of change, we must not hesitate to declare our ultimate objectives and to take concrete actions to move toward them. We must be staunch in our conviction that freedom is not the sole prerogative of a lucky few but the inalienable and universal right of all human beings. So states the United Nations Universal Declaration of Human Rights, which, among other things, guarantees free elections.

The objective I propose is quite simple to state: to foster the infrastructure of democracy, the system of a free press, unions, political parties, universities, which allows a people to choose their own way to develop their own culture, to reconcile their own differences through peaceful means.

This is not cultural imperialism; it is providing the means for genuine self-determination and protection for diversity. Democracy already flourishes in countries with very different cultures and historical experiences. It would be cultural condescension, or worse, to say that any people prefer dictatorship to democracy. Who would voluntarily choose not to have the right to vote, decide to purchase government propaganda handouts instead of independent newspapers, prefer government to worker-controlled unions, opt for land to be owned by the state instead of those who till it, want government repression of religious liberty, a single political party instead of a free choice, a rigid cultural orthodoxy instead of democratic tolerance and diversity?

The British people know that, given strong leadership, time, and a little bit of hope, the forces of good ultimately rally and triumph over evil. Here among you is the cradle of self-government, the mother of Parliaments. Here is the enduring greatness of the British contribution to mankind, the great civilized ideas: individual liberty, representative government, and the rule of law under God.

I've often wondered about the shyness of some of us in the West about standing for these ideals that have done so much to ease the plight of man and the hardships of our imperfect world. This reluctance to use those vast resources at our command reminds me of the elderly lady whose home was bombed in the blitz. As the rescuers moved about, they found a bottle of brandy she'd stored behind the staircase, which was all that was left standing. And since she was barely conscious, one of the workers pulled the cork to give her a taste of it. She came around immediately and said, "Here now—there now, put it back. That's for emergencies."

Well, the emergency is upon us. Let us be shy no longer. Let us go to our strength. Let us offer hope. Let us tell the world that a new age is not only possible but probable.

During the dark days of the Second World War, when this island was incandescent with courage, Winston Churchill exclaimed about Britain's adversaries, "What kind of people do they think we are?" Well, Britain's adversaries found out what extraordinary people the British are. But all the democracies paid a terrible price for allowing the dictators to underestimate us. We will not make that mistake again. So, let us ask ourselves, "What kind of people do we think we are?" And let us answer, "Free people, worthy of freedom and determined not only to remain so but to help others gain their freedom as well."

Sir Winston led his people to great victory in war and then lost an election just as the fruits of victory were about to be enjoyed. But he left office honorably and, as it turned out, temporarily, knowing that the liberty of his people was more important than the fate of any single leader. History recalls his greatness in ways no dictator will ever know. And he left us a message of hope for the future, as timely now as when he first uttered it, as opposition leader in the Commons nearly twenty-seven years ago, when he said, "When we look back on all the perils through which we have passed and at the mighty foes that we have laid low and all the dark and deadly designs that we have frustrated, why should we fear for our future? We have," he said, "come safely through the worst."

Well, the task I've set forth will long outlive our own generation. But together, we too have come through the worst. Let us now begin a major effort to secure the best—a crusade for freedom that will engage the faith and fortitude of the next generation. For the sake of peace and justice, let us move toward a world in which all people are at last free to determine their own destiny.

- Speech to the House of Commons, June 8, 1992

When God-Given Liberties Are Denied

During my lifetime, I have seen the rise of fascism and communism. Both philosophies glorify the arbitrary power of the state. These ideologies held, at first, a certain fascination for some intellectuals. But both theories fail. Both deny those God-given liberties that are the inalienable right of each person on this planet; indeed, they deny the existence of God. Because of this fundamental flaw, fascism has already been destroyed, and the bankruptcy of communism has been laid bare for all to see—a system that is efficient in producing machines of war but cannot feed its people.

-Remarks to Chinese community leaders
in Beijing, China, April 27, 1984

Remembering What Evil Looks Like

We gather here today, as we have been so eloquently told here, for a solemn, profound, saddening, and yet triumphant occasion. It's an occasion that commemorates all we've lost—the irreplaceable humanity whose monstrous end will ever testify to the hellish depths of human evil. But it's an occasion that commemorates something else as well, it commemorates the seriousness of our intention—as human beings, as Americans, and, in the case of many here today, as Jews—to keep the memory of the six million fresh and enduring.

We who did not go their way owe them this. We must make sure their deaths have posthumous meaning. We must make sure that from now until the end of days all humankind stares this evil in the face, that all humankind knows what this evil looks like and how it came to be. And when we truly know it for what it was, then and only then can we be sure that it will never come again.

Some people say evil of this degree is incomprehensible. They say we will never understand it. Some people even say that the word "evil" is insufficient to describe the Holocaust, and instead they use terms like mad, crazy, insane. I think they're wrong. What we saw there, at Treblinka and Belsen and Auschwitz and Dachau, was the image of the inferno. That may have been the ultimate purpose of those who made the Holocaust: a grotesque effort to hurl the Earth into the very pit of the serpent. I believe the Holocaust is comprehensible. Indeed, we must comprehend it. We have no choice; the future of mankind depends upon it. And that's what we're here for: to lay the cornerstone for the United States Holocaust Memorial Museum, which will help us understand and make it impossible for us to forget.

The Holocaust Memorial Council is committed to this purpose. It is composed of Republicans and Democrats and independents who understand that partisanship has no place here. There are Jews who serve on it and Catholics and Protestants, who understand that religious divisions have no place here. It is composed of those who came through the flames of the Holocaust and those who did not, for we've required no rules for membership except an unyielding commitment to our mission—to keep the memory alive.

To fulfill that mission, the museum will study the history of the Holocaust, provide an invaluable resource for researchers, and bring together in one place the greatest array of information and knowledge on this necessary subject. It will examine the nature and meaning of the continuing curse that is anti-Semitism. I think all of us here are aware of those, even among our own countrymen, who have dedicated themselves to the disgusting task of minimizing or even denying the truth of the Holocaust. This act of intellectual genocide must not go unchallenged, and those who advance these views must be held up to the scorn and wrath of all good and thinking people in this nation and across the world.

And yet just as we must challenge it here at home, so, too, we must challenge anti-Semitism abroad. We know that in certain nations an infamous and fraudulent document called the Protocols of the Elders of Zion is still being distributed and, in some cases, taught in school. This, the most profoundly cynical piece of anti-Semitic filth ever produced, is full of libels toward the Jewish people, particularly the horrifying "blood libel." We must send the message out to all the world: A blood libel against the Jewish people is a blood libel against all humankind, and no decent person will stand for it.

We know that the United Nations, whose peacekeepers were honored only last week for their service to the world, has yet to repeal its infamous resolution equating Zionism and racism. We know where such intellectual infamy can lead. The world has learned that when the truth is turned on its head, holocausts become possible.

And there are the subtler forms of anti-Semitism. There is the anti-Semitism that seeks to deny Jews their independent identity. In these days of *glasnost,* we hear talk about liberalizing attitudes toward Judaism in the Soviet Union. But it is still true that a Jew must have courage to rise and say with pride: "Yes, I am a Jew. I wish to study Hebrew, and I wish to emigrate to the homeland of my people." Those who speak those words know what follows them: the despair of waiting for permission to do that which is a basic human right—to go where they will when they choose. There are still tens of thousands—maybe even hundreds of thousands—of Soviet Jews who wait to leave the Soviet Union so that they may live free as Jews.

And here, as we lay this cornerstone and vow that the Jewish people will never stand alone against tyranny, I want to ask the Soviet leaders a question: Where are those exit visas? Where are they? And you and I and all Americans of good will are united in the challenge I propose to the Soviet leaders today. I say: Let these people go!

The Jews of silence, Elie Wiesel called them two decades ago, but they're silent no more. They're obeying what the great theologian Emil Fackenheim called the 614th Commandment—the Commandment of Auschwitz—and that commandment is this: "Let there be Jews." That commandment is dear to the hearts of all. The Jewish people were on this Earth at the time of the pyramids. Those structures are still standing, and the Jews are still here. We must make sure that when the tall towers of our greatest cities have crumbled to dust in the turnings of time, the Jewish people will still be on this Earth to cast their blessings and remind all of us that this world and the people who live upon it have a history and, yes, even a destiny.

This week we celebrate one of the worst anniversaries of this century. Last Friday, fifty years ago, the European nations met in Munich and accommodated the expansionist designs of Adolf Hitler. Prime Minister Neville Chamberlain returned to Britain and proclaimed that he had brought "peace for our time." And eleven months later the Nazi tanks rolled into Poland, and the war began. With the invasion of Poland the West awoke, may God be thanked, and the Nazis were finally defeated. But at what cost? At what cost?

Even to think about the cost makes sleep impossible. Had the West awakened to the meaning of Hitler, would those dead be with us today? Would there even be a need for this museum? It's

a question without an answer. But we must never allow ourselves to have to ask that question again. American troops who
liberated the concentration camps saw things no human eyes
should ever see. But if we in America remain strong—if we hold
fast and true to the conviction that, yes, there are things worth
fighting for, there are things worth dying for, and we will heed
the call if we must—humans will never suffer so nor will others
be called upon to save them from such suffering.

Before I go, I'd like to tell those of you who do not know it
already about a song that was sung in the camps. It was a
Yiddish song, and like many of the camp ballads, it was not
about the hunger and the torture and the dying but about the
coming of the Messiah. "What will happen," the song asks,
"when the Messiah comes?" And the answer is: "When the
Messiah comes, we'll have a banquet." And the banquet the
song describes is no ordinary repast. For at that Messianic banquet, the guests will eat of the creature called the Leviathan and
will drink the finest and sweetest wines. And they will sit and
watch while Miriam the prophetess dances for their entertainment. And then they will sit and listen as King David plays songs
for them on his harp. And they will sit and listen to a lecture
given by the wisest of men, King Solomon. And they will sit and
study the Torah with Moses.

I hope you'll forgive me if I say that I believe those who perished in the Holocaust have, after long suffering, attended that
banquet. I cannot imagine our Lord would deny their request.
We here will inscribe their names in human memory, and pray
that God may bless us all.

-Remarks at the site of the future Holocaust
Memorial Museum, October 5, 1988

When Governments Denounce God

The principles of wealth creation transcend time, people, and place. Governments that deliberately subvert them by denouncing God, smothering faith, destroying freedom, and confiscating wealth have impoverished their people. Communism works only in heaven, where they don't need it, and in hell, where they've already got it.

-Remarks at the National Conference of the
National Federation of Independent Business,
June 22, 1983

The Evil of Bigotry

A few years ago ... I noted that there was sin and evil in the world and that all of us had a spiritual obligation to fight it. This was interpreted by a few to mean opposition to totalitarian and communist dictators. Well, of course, that's true. But the real context of the quote is rarely given. I was talking specifically then about America's own spiritual problems.... America, too, has what I call "a legacy of evil" to contend with, things like racism or anti-Semitism or other forms of intolerance.... That's what America is all about: freedom, tolerance, each different religious and racial group looking out for the rights of the other. And I think this is a good theme for all of us to reflect upon as we worship and give thanks to the Lord. Let us pray that America will always use her power wisely, justly, and humbly to defend our legitimate interests, to help those who are struggling for freedom. But let us pray too that

God will give our country the humility to see our own faults and the strength to preserve our hard-won tradition of freedom to worship and religious tolerance.

-Radio address to nation, March 29, 1986

4 | PROTECTING THE SANCTITY OF LIFE

> To diminish the value of one category of
> human life is to diminish us all. – 1984

The Most Basic Human Right

We must do our duty to generations not yet born. We cannot proclaim the noble ideal that human life is sacred, then turn our backs on the taking of some four thousand unborn children's lives every day. This as a means of birth control must stop.

In a recent speech to the National Religious Broadcasters, I stated that as abortions are performed, the unborn children that are being killed often feel excruciating pain. And, oh, immediately, that statement prompted sharp criticism and denials. Well, just the other day, I received a letter signed by twenty-four medical doctors, including such eminent physicians as Dr. Bernie Pisani, president of the New York State Medical Society, and Dr. Anne Bannon, former chief of pediatrics at the St. Louis City Hospital. The letter explained that in recent years medical techniques have "demonstrated the remarkable responsiveness of the human fetus to pain, touch, and sound." "Mr. President," the letter concluded, "in drawing attention to the capability of the human fetus to feel pain, you stand on firmly established ground."

Many who seek abortions do so in harrowing circumstances. Often, they suffer deep personal trauma. Just as tolerance means accepting that many in good faith hold views different from our own, it also means that no man or woman should sit in judgment on another. If we could rise above bitterness and reproach, if Americans could come together in a spirit of understanding and helping, then we could find positive solutions to the tragedy of abortion—and this we must do.

The values and freedoms we cherish as Americans rest on our fundamental commitment to the sanctity of human life. The first of the "inalienable rights" affirmed by our Declaration of Independence is the right to life itself, a right the Declaration states has been endowed by our Creator on all human beings—whether young or old, weak or strong, healthy or handicapped.

Since 1973, however, more than fifteen million unborn children have died in legalized abortions—a tragedy of stunning dimensions that stands in sad contrast to our belief that each life is sacred. These children, over tenfold the number of Americans lost in all our nation's wars, will never laugh, never sing, never experience the joy of human love; nor will they strive to heal the sick, or feed the poor, or make peace among nations. Abortion has denied them the first and most basic of human rights, and we are infinitely poorer for their loss.

We are poorer not simply for lives not led and for contributions not made, but also for the erosion of our sense of the worth and dignity of every individual. To diminish the value of one category of human life is to diminish us all. Slavery, which treated blacks as something less than human, to be bought and sold if convenient, cheapened human life and mocked our dedication to the freedom and equality of all men and women. Can we say that abortion—which treats the unborn as something less than human, to be destroyed if convenient—will be less corrosive to the values we hold dear?

We have been given the precious gift of human life, made more precious still by our births in or pilgrimages to a land of freedom. It is fitting, then, on the anniversary of the Supreme Court decision in *Roe v. Wade* that struck down state anti-abortion laws, that we reflect anew on these blessings, and on our corresponding responsibility to guard with care the lives and freedoms of even the weakest of our fellow human beings....

-Proclamation, National Sanctity
of Human Life Day, 1984

Abortion and the Conscience of the Nation

Abortion concerns not just the unborn child, it concerns every one of us. The English poet, John Donne, wrote: "Any man's death diminishes me, because I am involved in mankind; and therefore never send to know for whom the bell tolls; it tolls for thee." We cannot diminish the value of one category of human life—the unborn—without diminishing the value of all human life.... The cultural environment for a human holocaust is present whenever any society can be misled into defining individuals as less than human and therefore devoid of value and respect. As a nation today, we have not rejected the sanctity of human life. The American people have not had an opportunity to express their view on the sanctity of human life in the unborn. I am convinced that Americans do not want to play God with the value of human life. It is not for us to decide who is worthy to live and who is not. Even the Supreme Court's opinion in *Roe v. Wade* did not explicitly reject the traditional American idea of intrinsic worth and value in all human life; it simply dodged the issue....

I have often said we need to join in prayer to bring protection to the unborn. Prayer and action are needed to uphold the sanctity of human life. I believe it will not be possible to accomplish our work, the work of saving lives, without being a soul of prayer. The famous British member of Parliament William Wilberforce prayed with his small group of influential friends, the "Clapham Sect," for decades to see an end to slavery in the British empire. Wilberforce led that struggle in Parliament, unflaggingly, because he believed in the sanctity of human life. He saw the fulfillment of this impossible dream when Parliament outlawed slavery just before his death. Let his faith and perseverance be our guide. We will never recognize the true value of our own lives until we affirm the value of others, a value of which Malcolm Muggeridge says: "However low it flickers or fiercely burns, it is still Divine flame which no man dare presume to put out, be his motives ever so humane and enlightened."

- *Abortion and the Conscience of the Nation* (1984).

Human Dignity in the Sight of God

Reverence for human life and recognition of the sanctity of individual life are among the defining characteristics of a just civil order. For century upon century, mankind has struggled to establish such principles in law—not merely as right ideas confirmable by experience, but as self-evident truths that provide the only possible basis for the creation of durable political institutions. Age after age of wars and persecutions, serfdom and slavery, have left bitter reminders of the consequences that everywhere follow a failure to recognize the fundamental dignity and equality of human beings in the sight of God.

Our nation was born in the midst of a struggle in which these principles were the real field of battle. The United States of America was founded by visionary people who believed, and said forthrightly, that the test of any just political system lay in whether it affirmed the inalienable rights endowed by God, rights that no civil authority was ever free to deny or contravene. In this context, it is no wonder then that the first right proclaimed by our founders in the Declaration of Independence was that of life, and that the care of human life and happiness, as Jefferson declared in words now inscribed on the marble walls of our national memorial to him, was held to be the first and only legitimate object of good government.

Today our nation, economically prosperous and at peace, bears a fresh, dark wound upon its conscience, a wound created by a stark deviation from the course of our national journey. Contrary to the purpose of law, to the character of medicine, to the habit of charity, and to the spirit of our founding, abortion has become routinized in America. No one can mistake abortion for the gentle art of healing. Each day in our land the promise of life is stolen from thousands of the unborn, the first flower of their unique existence crushed forever. But, as many philosophers have pointed out, the effects of such acts of violence are just as profound on those who perform them as on those who undergo them.

Americans are a generous and kindhearted people, a people who strive to strengthen and preserve those delicate bonds of affection that unite the human family and give safe harbor to all its members. We often fail in our tenderness and mercy; but it is not in our nature to choose failure. Rather, we are a people who thirst after justice and will give our all to achieve it and defend it. Most particularly, we are a people who will not settle for a national policy that each year condemns 1.5 million unborn children to an early death and consigns their mothers to exploitation and emptiness. We must and we will answer abortion with loving alternatives like adoption, and we will ensure that our laws preserve and protect the innocent unborn from destruction.

In 1989 America can make a new beginning as a champion of the most basic civil right of all. We can, as is written in Deuteronomy, choose life, so that we and our descendants may live....

-Proclamation 5931, National Sanctity
of Human Life Day, 1989

Such Is the Kingdom of God

I know what I'm about to say now is controversial, but I have to say it. This nation cannot continue turning a blind eye and a deaf ear to the taking of some four thousand unborn children's lives every day. That's one every twenty-one seconds. One every twenty-one seconds.

This nation fought a terrible war so that black Americans would be guaranteed their God-given rights. Abraham Lincoln recognized that we could not survive as a free land when some could decide whether others should be free or slaves. Well, today another question begs to be asked: How can we survive as a free nation when some decide that others are not fit to live and should be done away with?

I believe no challenge is more important to the character of America than restoring the right to life to all human beings. Without that right, no other rights have meaning. "Suffer the little children to come unto me, and forbid them not, for such is the kingdom of God" (see Mk 10:14).

I will continue to support every effort to restore that protection, including the Hyde-Jepsen respect life bill. I've asked for your all-out commitment, for the mighty power of your prayers, so that together we can convince our fellow countrymen that America should, can, and will preserve God's greatest gift.

-Remarks, Annual Convention of the National
Religious Broadcasters, January 30, 1984

In Defense of the Child

If you came upon an immobile body and you yourself could not determine whether it was dead or alive, I think that you would decide to consider it alive until somebody could prove it was dead. You wouldn't get a shovel and start covering it up. And I think we should do the same thing with regard to abortion.

-Remark to reporter, White House
press conference, January 19, 1982

5 | PATRIOTISM IN A DEMOCRATIC SOCIETY

> Should Moses have told the children of Israel
> to live in slavery rather than dare the wilder-
> ness? Should Christ have refused the cross?
> Should the patriots at Concord Bridge have
> refused to fire the shot heard 'round the
> world? Are we to believe that all the martyrs
> of the world die in vain? – 1964

The Miracle of Freedom

Some years ago a writer, who happened to be an avid student of history, told me a story about that day in the little hall in Philadelphia where honorable men, hard-pressed by a king who was flouting the very law they were willing to obey, debated whether they should take the fateful step of declaring their independence from that king. I was told by this man that the story could be found in the writings of Jefferson. I confess, I never researched or made an effort to verify it. Perhaps it is only legend. But, story or legend, he described the atmosphere, the strain, the debate, and that as men for the first time faced the consequences of such an irretrievable act, the walls resounded with the dread word of treason and its price—the gallows and the headman's axe. As the day wore on the issue hung in the balance, and then, according to the story, a man rose in the small gallery. He was not a young man and was obviously calling on all the energy he could muster. Citing the grievances that had brought them to this moment he said, "Sign that parchment. They may turn every tree into a gallows, every home into a grave and yet the words of that parchment can never die. For the mechanic in his workshop, they will be words of hope, to the slave in the mines—freedom." And he added, "If my hands were freezing in death, I would sign that parchment with my last ounce of strength. Sign, sign if the next moment the noose is around your neck, sign even if the hall is ringing with the sound of the headman's axe, for that parchment will be the textbook of freedom, the bible of the rights of man forever." And then, it is said, he fell back exhausted. But fifty-six delegates, swept by his eloquence, signed the Declaration of Independence, a document destined to be as immortal as any work of man can be. And according to the story, when they turned to thank him for his timely oratory, he could not be found nor were there any who knew who he was or how he had come in or gone out through the locked and guarded doors.

Well, as I say, whether story or legend, the signing of the document that day in Independence Hall was miracle enough. Fifty-six men, a little band so unique—we have never seen their like since—pledged their lives, their fortunes, and their sacred honor. Sixteen gave their lives, most gave their fortunes, and all of them preserved their sacred honor. What manner of men were they? Certainly they were not unwashed, revolutionary rebels, nor were they adventurers in a heroic mood. Twenty-four were lawyers and jurists, eleven were merchants and tradesmen, nine were farmers. They were men who would achieve security but valued freedom more.

And what price did they pay? John Hart was driven from the side of his desperately ill wife. After more than a year of living almost as an animal in the forest and in caves, he returned to find his wife had died and his children had vanished. He never saw them again, his property was destroyed, and he died of a broken heart—but with no regret, only pride in the part he had played that day in Independence Hall. Carter Braxton of Virginia lost all his ships—they were sold to pay his debts. He died in rags. So it was with Ellery, Clymer, Hall, Walton, Gwinnett, Rutledge, Morris, Livingston, and Middleton. Nelson, learning that Cornwallis was using his home for a head-quarters, personally begged Washington to fire on him and destroy his home—he died bankrupt. It has never been re-ported that any of these men ever expressed bitterness or renounced their action as not worth the price. Fifty-six rank-and-file, ordinary citizens had founded a nation that grew from sea to shining sea, five million farms, quiet villages, cities that never sleep—all done without an area redevelopment plan, urban renewal, or a rural legal assistance program.

Now we are a nation of 211 million people with a pedigree that includes bloodlines from every corner of the world. We have shed that American-melting-pot blood in every corner of the world, usually in defense of someone's freedom. Those who remained of that remarkable band we call our Founding Fathers tied up some of the loose ends about a dozen years after the Revolution. It had been the first revolution in all man's history that did not just exchange one set of rulers for another. This had been a philosophical revolution. The culmination of men's dreams for six thousand years were formalized with the

Constitution, probably the most unique document ever drawn in the long history of man's relation to man. I know there have been other constitutions, and new ones are being drawn today by newly emerging nations. Most of them, even the one of the Soviet Union, contain many of the same guarantees as our own Constitution, and still there is a difference. The difference is so subtle that we often overlook it, but it is so great that it tells the whole story. Those other constitutions say, "Government grants you these rights" and ours says, "You are born with these rights, they are yours by the grace of God, and no government on Earth can take them from you."

Lord Acton of England, who once said, "Power corrupts, and absolute power corrupts absolutely," would say of that document, "They had solved with astonishing ease and unduplicated success two problems which had heretofore baffled the capacity of the most enlightened nations. They had contrived a system of federal government which prodigiously increased national power and yet respected local liberties and authorities, and they had founded it on a principle of equality without surrendering the securities of property or freedom." Never in any society has the preeminence of the individual been so firmly established and given such a priority.

In less than twenty years we would go to war because the God-given rights of the American sailors, as defined in the Constitution, were being violated by a foreign power. We served notice then on the world that all of us together would act collectively to safeguard the rights of even the least among us. But still, in an older, cynical world, they were not convinced. The great powers of Europe still had the idea that one day this great continent would be open again to colonizing and they would came over and divide us up.

In the meantime, men who yearned to breathe free were making their way to our shores. Among them was a young refugee from the Austro-Hungarian Empire. He had been a leader in an attempt to free Hungary from Austrian rule. The attempt had failed and he fled to escape execution. In America, this young Hungarian, Koscha by name, became an importer by trade and took out his first citizenship papers. One day, business took him to a Mediterranean port. There was a large Austrian warship under the command of an admiral in the harbor. He had a manservant with him. He had described to this manservant what the flag of his new country looked like. Word was passed to the Austrian warship that this revolutionary was there and in the night he was kidnapped and taken aboard that large ship. This man's servant, desperate, walking up and down the harbor, suddenly spied a flag that resembled the description he had heard. It was a small American war sloop. He went aboard and told Captain Ingraham, of that war sloop, his story. Captain Ingraham went to the American consul. When the American consul learned that Koscha had only taken out his first citizenship papers, the consul washed his hands of the incident. Captain Ingraham said, "I am the senior officer in this port and I believe, under the oath of my office, that I owe this man the protection of our flag."

He went aboard the Austrian warship and demanded to see their prisoner, our citizen. The admiral was amused, but they brought the man on deck. He was in chains and had been badly beaten. Captain Ingraham said, "I can hear him better without those chains," and the chains were removed. He walked over and said to Koscha, "I will ask you one question; consider your answer carefully. Do you ask the protection of the American flag?" Koscha nodded dumbly "Yes," and the captain said, "You shall have it." He went back and told the frightened consul what he had done. Later in the day three more Austrian ships sailed into harbor. It looked as though the four were getting ready to leave. Captain Ingraham sent a junior officer over to the Austrian flagship to tell the admiral that any attempt to leave that harbor with our citizen aboard would be resisted with appropriate force. He said that he would expect a satisfactory answer by four o'clock that afternoon. As the hour neared they looked at each other through the glasses. As it struck four he had them roll the cannons into the ports and had them light the tapers with which they would set off the cannons—one little sloop. Suddenly the lookout tower called out and said, "They are lowering a boat," and they rowed Koscha over to the little American ship.

Captain Ingraham then went below and wrote his letter of resignation to the United States Navy. In it he said, "I did what I thought my oath of office required, but if I have embarrassed my country in any way, I resign." His resignation was refused in the United States Senate with these words: "This battle that was never fought may turn out to be the most important battle in our nation's history." Incidentally, there is to this day, and I hope there always will be, a USS Ingraham in the United States Navy.

-Remarks at the Conservative Political
Action Committee, January 25, 1974

The Goodness of America

I feel duty-bound to inform you that I am going to try to give you some remarks from my mind and heart; but they certainly will not be an address. If I had a text for anything I am going to say, you have heard it in the opening hymn, "America the Beautiful." I know that this is not particularly a fashionable subject. Too many tub-thumping politicians on too many Fourths of July have paid word tribute in platitudes to the Fourth of July speech and waved the flag. All of us as we grow older have a tendency to grow a little more cynical, to find fault, to see the things that should be done and as we're younger we're a little impatient with sentiment and emotion. We are a little reluctant to show it, we're impatient for change, and we want correction of those things that are wrong and should be done and so, perhaps, none of us pay enough attention to the very thought behind this land of ours....

America is less of a place than an idea, and if it is an idea, and I believe that to be true, it is an idea that has been deep in the souls of man ever since man started his long trail from the swamps. It is nothing but the inherent love of freedom in each one of us, and the great ideological struggle that we find ourselves engaged in today is not a new struggle. It's the same old battle. We met it under the name of Hitlerism; we met it under the name of Kaiserism; and we have met it back through the ages in the name of every conqueror that has ever set upon a course of establishing his rule over mankind. It is simply the idea, the basis of this country and of our religion, the idea of the dignity of man, the idea that deep within the heart of each one of us is something so godlike and precious that no individual or group has a right to impose his or its will upon the people, that no group can decide for the people what is good for the people so well as they can decide for themselves.

I, in my own mind, have thought of America as a place in the divine scheme of things that was set aside as a promised land. It was set here and the price of admission was very simple; the means of selection was very simple as to how this land should be populated. Any place in the world and any person from those places; any person with the courage, with the desire to tear up the roots, to strive for freedom, to attempt and dare to live in a strange and foreign place, to travel half across the world was welcome here. And they have brought with them to the blood-stream that has become America that precious courage, the courage that they, and they alone in their community, in their nation, in their family, had in the first place, to this land, the hometown, to strive for something better for themselves and for their children and their children's children. I believe that God in shedding his grace on this country has always in this divine scheme of things kept an eye on our land and guided it as a promised land for these people.

-Commencement address, William Woods College,
Fulton, Missouri, June 1952

The Sacrifice of Freedom-Loving People

We stand today at a place of battle, one that forty years ago saw and felt the worst of war. Men bled and died here for a few feet—or inches—of sand, as bullets and shellfire cut through their ranks. About them, General Omar Bradley later said,

"Every man who set foot on Omaha Beach that day was a hero."

Some who survived the battle of June 6, 1944, are here today. Others who hoped to return never did.

"Someday, Lis, I'll go back," said Private First Class Peter Robert Zannata, of the 37th Engineer Combat Battalion, and first assault wave to hit Omaha Beach. "I'll go back and I'll see it all again. I'll see the beach, the barricades, and the graves."

Those words of Private Zannata come to us from his daughter, Lisa Zannata Henn, in a heartrending story about the event her father spoke of so often. "In his words, the Normandy invasion would change his life forever," she said. She tells some of his stories of World War II but says of her father, "the story to end all stories was D-Day."

"He made me feel the fear of being on the boat waiting to land. I can smell the ocean and feel the seasickness. I can see the looks on his fellow soldiers' faces—the fear, the anguish, the uncertainty of what lay ahead. And when they landed, I can feel the strength and courage of the men who took those first steps through the tide to what must have surely looked like instant death."

Private Zannata's daughter wrote to me, "I don't know how or why I can feel this emptiness, this fear, or this determination, but I do. Maybe it's the bond I had with my father. All I know is that it brings tears to my eyes to think about my father as a twenty-year-old boy having to face that beach."

The anniversary of D-Day was always special to her family. And like all the families of those who went to war, she describes how she came to realize her own father's survival was a miracle: "So many men died. I know that my father watched many of his friends be killed. I know that he must have died inside a little each time. But his explanation to me was, 'You did what you had to do, and you kept on going.'"

When men like Private Zannata and all our Allied forces stormed the beaches of Normandy forty years ago they came not as conquerors, but as liberators. When these troops swept across the French countryside and into the forests of Belgium and Luxembourg they came not to take, but to return what had been wrongfully seized. When our forces marched into Germany they came not to prey on a brave and defeated people, but to nurture the seeds of democracy among those who yearned to be free again.

We salute them today. But, Mr. President [François Mitterand of France], we also saw those who, like yourself, were already engaging the enemy inside your beloved country—the French Resistance. Your valiant struggle for France did so much to cripple the enemy and spur the advance of the armies of liberation. The French Forces of the Interior will forever personify courage and national spirit. They will be a timeless inspiration to all who are free and to all who would be free.

Today, in their memory, and for all who fought here, we celebrate the triumph of democracy. We reaffirm the unity of democratic people who fought a war and then joined with the vanquished in a firm resolve to keep the peace.

From a terrible war we learned that unity made us invincible; now, in peace, that same unity makes us secure. We sought to bring all freedom-loving nations together in a community dedicated to the defense and preservation of our sacred values. Our alliance, forged in the crucible of war, tempered and shaped by the realities of the postwar world, has succeeded. In Europe, the threat has been contained, the peace has been kept.

Today, the living here assembled—officials, veterans, citizens—are a tribute to what was achieved here forty years ago. This land is secure. We are free. These things are worth fighting and dying for.

Lisa Zannata Henn began her story by quoting her father, who promised that he would return to Normandy. She ended with a promise to her father, who died eight years ago of cancer: "I'm going there, Dad, and I'll see the beaches and the barricades and the monuments. I'll see the graves, and I'll put flowers there just like you wanted to do. I'll never forget what you went through, Dad, nor will I let anyone else forget. And, Dad, I'll always be proud."

Through the words of his loving daughter, who is here with us today, a D-Day veteran has shown us the meaning of this day far better than any president can. It is enough to say about Private Zannata and all the men of honor and courage who fought beside him four decades ago: We will always remember. We will always be proud. We will always be prepared, so we may always be free.

-Address at Omaha Beach (Normandy, France),
fortieth anniversary of D-Day, June 6, 1984

Faith in a Merciful God

We're here to mark that day in history when the Allied peoples joined in battle to reclaim this continent to liberty. For four long years, much of Europe had been under a terrible shadow. Free nations had fallen, Jews cried out in the camps, millions cried out for liberation. Europe was enslaved, and the world prayed for its rescue. Here in Normandy the rescue began. Here the Allies stood and fought against tyranny in a giant undertaking unparalleled in human history.

We stand on a lonely, windswept point on the northern shore of France. The air is soft, but forty years ago at this moment, the air was dense with smoke and the cries of men, and the air was filled with the crack of rifle fire and the roar of cannons. At dawn, on the morning of the sixth of June, 1944, 225 Rangers jumped off the British landing craft and ran to the bottom of these cliffs. Their mission was one of the most difficult and daring of the invasion: to climb these sheer and desolate cliffs and take out the enemy guns. The Allies had been told that some of the mightiest of these guns were here and they would be trained on the beaches to stop the Allied advance.

The Rangers looked up and saw the enemy soldiers—at the edge of the cliff shooting down at them with machine guns and throwing grenades. And the American Rangers began to climb. They shot rope ladders over the face of these cliffs and began to pull themselves up. When one Ranger fell, another would take his place. When one rope was cut, a Ranger would grab another and begin his climb again. They climbed, shot back, and held their footing. Soon, one by one, the Rangers pulled themselves over the top, and in seizing the firm land at the top of these cliffs, they began to seize back the continent of Europe. Two hundred and twenty-five came here. After two days of fighting, only ninety could still bear arms.

Behind me is a memorial that symbolizes the Ranger daggers that were thrust into the top of these cliffs. And before me are the men who put them there.

These are the boys of Pointe du Hoc. These are the men who took the cliffs. These are the champions who helped free a continent. These are the heroes who helped end a war.

Gentlemen, I look at you and I think of Stephen Spender's poem. You are men who in your "lives fought for life ... and left the vivid air signed with your honor...."

Forty summers have passed since the battle that you fought here. You were young the day you took these cliffs; some of you were hardly more than boys, with the deepest joys of life before you. Yet you risked everything here. Why? Why did you do it? What impelled you to put aside the instinct for self-preservation and risk your lives to take these cliffs? What inspired all the men of the armies that met here? We look at you, and somehow we know the answer. It was faith, and belief; it was loyalty and love.

The men of Normandy had faith that what they were doing was right, faith that they fought for all humanity, faith that a just God would grant them mercy on this beachhead or on the next. It was the deep knowledge—and pray God we have not lost it— that there is a profound moral difference between the use of force for liberation and the use of force for conquest. You were here to liberate, not to conquer, and so you and those others did not doubt your cause. And you were right not to doubt.

You all know that some things are worth dying for. One's country is worth dying for, and democracy is worth dying for, because it's the most deeply honorable form of government ever devised by man. All of you loved liberty. All of you were willing to fight tyranny, and you knew the people of your countries were behind you.

-Address at Pointe du Hoc, Normandy,
June 6, 1984

True Patriotism

True patriotism is a love of country, but it must be an intelligent love and not blind devotion to one's nation without regard to its ideals. Abraham Lincoln recognized this when, speaking in tribute of Henry Clay, he said:

"He loved his country partly because it was his own country, but mostly because it was a free country; and he burned with a zeal for its advancement, prosperity, and glory, because he saw in such, the advancement, prosperity, and glory of human liberty, human right, and human nature."

The patriotism of Clay, Lincoln, and generations of Americans was of this nature. They loved their country because it was theirs but even more because it was a land where liberty, justice, and opportunity flourished. They did not love it because of its government but because of its people; not because of the role its government played in world affairs but because of the inspiration the very idea of America gave to every person, great and small, who made this blessed land his home, and to every person in the less fortunate lands of the world who, amid oppression, tyranny, and injustice—as in Poland today—looked to America as the land of freedom.

Americans today should dedicate themselves again to that true patriotism. We should dedicate ourselves again to the enduring values of family, neighborhood, work, peace, and freedom which have characterized our country these past two centuries. Let us do this, and our patriotism will be strong and fulfilling.

-A proclamation, National Patriotism Week,
February 18, 1982

The Banner of Freedom

As we think back over the history of our nation's flag, we remember that the story of its early years was often one of hardship and trials, sometimes a fight for simple survival.

Such is the story behind our Star-Spangled Banner. It was two years into the War of 1812, and America seemed to be teetering on the edge of defeat. The British had already taken our capital and burned the White House. Baltimore was the next target in a grand design to divide our forces and crush this newly independent nation of upstart colonies. All that stood between the British and Baltimore were the guns of Fort McHenry, blocking their entry into Baltimore Harbor.

The British bombardment lasted for twenty-five hours. Through the dark hours of the night, the rockets fired and the bombs exploded. And a young American patriot named Key, held captive aboard a British ship, watched anxiously for some proof, some sign, that liberty would prevail. You can imagine his joy when the next morning, in the dawn's early light, he looked out and saw the banner still flying—a little tattered and torn, but still flying proudly above the ramparts. Fort McHenry and the brave men manning it had withstood the assault. Baltimore was saved. The United States, this great experiment in human freedom, as George Washington described it, would endure.

Thinking back to those times, one realizes that our democracy is so strong because it was forged in the fires of adversity. In those dark days of the war, it must have been easy to give in to despair. But our forefathers were motivated by a cause beyond themselves. From the harsh winter of Valley Forge to the blazing night above Fort McHenry, those patriot soldiers were sustained by the ideals of human freedom. Through the hardships and the setbacks, they kept their eyes on that ideal and purpose, just as through the smoke of battle they kept a lookout for the flag. For with the birth of our nation, the cause of human freedom had become forever tied to that flag and its survival.

As the American republic grew and prospered and new stars were added to the flag, the ideal of freedom grew and prospered. From the rolling hills of Kentucky to the shores of California to the Sea of Tranquility on the moon, our pioneers carried our flag before them, a symbol of the indomitable spirit of a free people. And let us never forget that in honoring our flag, we honor the American men and women who have courageously fought and died for it over the last two hundred years, patriots who set an ideal above any consideration of self. Our flag flies free today because of their sacrifice.

And I hope you all will join Nancy and me and millions of other Americans at seven o'clock this evening, Eastern Daylight Time, when we pause a few minutes to say the Pledge of Allegiance. Though separated by many miles, we will be together in our thoughts. These anniversaries remind us that the great American experiment in freedom and democracy has really just begun. They remind us of the terrible hardships our forefathers willingly endured for their beliefs. And they challenge us to match that greatness of spirit in our own time, and I know we will. We are, after all, the land of the free and the home of the brave....

-Radio address, July 4, 1986

Freedom Fighters

It is, in a way, an odd thing to honor those who died in defense of our country, in defense of us, in wars far away. The imagination plays a trick. The imagination sees these soldiers in our mind as old and wise. We see them as something like a Founding Father, grave and gray-haired. But most of them were boys when they died, and they gave up two lives—the one they were living and the one they would have lived. When they died, they gave up their chances to be husbands and fathers and grandfathers. They gave up their chance to be revered old men. They gave up everything for our country, for us. And all we can do is remember.

- Remarks at Arlington National Cemetery,
November 11, 1985

6 | RESTORATION OF THE FAMILY

> We fear the government may be powerful
> enough to destroy our families;
> we know that is is not powerful enough
> to replace them. – 1977

Making Old Values New

I happen to think that it's always hard to be young. The young are so vulnerable and often feel misunderstood. But the children and teenagers and young adults our society has produced the last twenty years or so seem in some ways to have had it harder than many of us older folks did. We grew up in a different America—an America of small towns and big families; an America where generations lived together and lines of authority, both within the home and outside it, were clear. We did not, for whatever reasons, question the premises of life so much. It seemed a more secure age.

But the world is changing. And the facts of our life have changed. Throughout our history we've relied on the family as the principal institution for transmitting values. But these days the American family is very different from what it was. Many families are headed by a single parent. Families are smaller, not only with fewer children but with fewer generations living together. The extended family is increasingly a thing of the past, and so is the old tradition of generation after generation living in the same town and the same house.

We're a country on the move. We're wed to mobility, and the ties that bind us seem looser. We watch a lot of television, seeking continuity and reassurance in the regular and predictable appearance of our favorite TV stars and programs. They visit us—as if they were a friend or relative coming by for the evening. TV is increasingly becoming the American neighbor. And the fact that it serves that function reflects what it is that we're missing.

The point I'm making is that we're an America of changing institutions and changing traditions. And change can be difficult, especially for young people.

In the sixties, the first generation to completely feel the assault of modern life almost came apart. Our youth seemed disoriented. But now, in the eighties, when some would have thought that things would be worse, they seem better. The young people of today are so solid, so alive to the good things in life, the deepest pleasure. They seem to care about the things worth caring about.

The polls show they're intensely patriotic. And they're very interested in home, career, and family—all of the things that go into creating what we call society.

You saw the Olympic athletes a few weeks ago—teenagers, many of them. You saw that they had faith in themselves; faith that great effort will be rewarded, that trying to improve your talents is worth it. You saw the love of country that they displayed with a shining lack of self-consciousness.

Somehow amidst all this change, all this movement, our

young people have held on. What we're seeing, I think, is a reappreciation of our sense of national roots; a reappreciation of the traditions and values our country lived by; a reappreciation of the things that give us a sense of continuity, a sense that there is a purpose to life. And many of our young people seem to be doing it on their own, as if they're personally rediscovering these things and making them new again.

I'm not talking about nostalgia for the past, but refinding what worked about the past and bringing it into the present and the future. Refinding our bearings, forging a sense of continuity where it doesn't exist outwardly in the facts of our lives, we have to recreate connections—connections with our family, between the family and the community. We need guideposts to help us find the way. And all this will evolve as we bring the best along with us.

People wonder why there's such a feeling of hope these days, and they come up with reasons—oh, the stock market's up, inflation is down. That's only a part of it. I think we're feeling hope again because we're taking old values and making them new....

-Remarks at a ceremony for the Young American
Medals for Bravery, August 28, 1984

The Centrality of the Family

Family life and the life of freedom are interdependent. In the arena of the family, children learn the most important lessons they will ever receive about their inherent dignity as individuals. They learn as well about the social and religious traditions that unite generation to generation, and they begin to acquire the values for which their ancestors sacrificed so much for freedom.

The centrality of the family is acknowledged even by those forces that would weaken or destroy it. Totalitarian societies see in the family a natural enemy, a bulwark of basic loyalties and inherited ideals that places allegiance in relationships that precede the claims of the state. Corrosive influences such as illegal drugs and pornography seek to substitute for the permanent bonds of family life a transient and ultimately false sense of happiness and fulfillment. Against these forces the family can often seem helpless and ineffective, but experience shows that it is in being tested that the strength of the family finally reveals itself. After all, the family has been with us from the dawn of human history, and there is no reason to believe that it will not endure.

National Family Week affords all Americans the opportunity to frankly face and assess the quality of family life in our nation and to reflect on what each of us can do as a father, daughter, mother, son, or grandparent—as a member of a family—to strengthen this divine institution. Better yet, let us undertake this reflection as families and as a family of free people. As Chesterton said, "The family is the test of freedom." Let us make this another test America refuses to fail.

- A proclamation, National Family Week,
November 21, 1986

Preserving the Family

The family is the basic unit of our society, the heart of our free democracy. It provides love, acceptance, guidance, support, and instruction to the individual. Community values and goals that give America strength also take root in the home. In times of change and challenge, families keep safe our cultural heritage and reinforce our spiritual foundation.

As the mainstay of our national life, family life must be preserved. When a family needs external assistance to help it to perform its unique role, this assistance should not interfere with the family's fundamental responsibilities and prerogatives. Rather, aid should be supportive and purposeful in strengthening the family's stability, self-sufficiency, and permanence....

Let us pledge that our institutions and policies will be shaped to enhance an environment in which families can strengthen their ties and best exercise their beliefs, authority, and resourcefulness. And let us make our pledge mindful that we do so not only on behalf of individual family members, but for America.

-A proclamation, National Family Week,
November 3, 1981

Keeping Families Together

My fellow Americans: This is a very special time of year for us, a time for family reunions and for celebrating together the blessings of God and the promises He has given us. From Thanksgiving to Hanukkah, which our Jewish community is now celebrating, to Christmas in three weeks' time, this is a season of hope and of love.

Certainly one of the greatest blessings for people everywhere is the family itself. The American Family Institute recently dedicated its book of essays, *The Family in the Modern World,* to Maria Victoria Walesa, daughter of Danuta and Lech Walesa, to whose christening came seven thousand Poles expressing their belief that the family remains the foundation of freedom. And, of course, they're right. It's in the family where we learn to think for ourselves, care for others, and acquire the values of self-reliance, integrity, responsibility, and compassion.

Families stand at the center of society, so building our future must begin by preserving family values. Tragically, too many in Washington have been asking us to swallow a whopper: namely, that bigger government is the greatest force for fairness and progress. But this so-called solution has given most of us a bad case of financial indigestion. How can families survive when big government's powers to tax, inflate, and regulate absorb their wealth, usurp their rights, and crush their spirit? As economic and social pressures have increased, the bonds that bind families together have come under strain. For example, three times as many families are headed by single parents today as in 1960. Many single parents make heroic sacrifices and deserve all our support. But there is no question that many well-intentioned Great Society-type programs contributed to family breakups, welfare dependency, and a large increase in births out of wedlock. In the 1970s the number of single mothers rose from 8 to 13 percent among whites and from 31 to a tragic 47 percent among blacks. Too often their children grow up poor, malnourished, and lacking in motivation. It's a path to social and health problems, low school performance, unemployment, and delinquency.

If we strengthen families, we'll help reduce poverty and the whole range of other social problems.

We can begin by reducing the economic burdens of inflation and taxes, and we're doing this. Since 1980 inflation has been chopped by three-fourths. Taxes have been cut for every family that earns a living, and we've increased the tax credit for child care. Yesterday we learned that our growing economy reduced unemployment to 8.2 percent last month. The payroll employment figure went up by 370,000 jobs.

At the same time, new policies are helping our neediest families move from dependence to independence. Our new job training law will train over a million needy and unemployed Americans each year for productive jobs. I should add that our enterprise zones proposal would stimulate new businesses, bringing jobs and hope to some of the most destitute areas of the country. The Senate has adopted this proposal. But after two years of delay, the House Democratic leadership only recently agreed to hold its first hearing on the legislation. This is a jobs bill America needs. And come January, we expect action.

We're moving forward on many other fronts. We've made prevention of drug abuse among youth a top priority. We'll soon announce a national missing children's center to help find and rescue children who've been abducted and exploited. We're working with states and local communities to increase the adoption of special-needs children. More children with permanent homes mean fewer children with permanent problems.

We're also stiffening the enforcement of child support from

absent parents. And we're trying hard to improve education through more discipline, a return to the basics, and through reforms like tuition tax credits to help hardworking parents.

In coming months, we'll propose new ways to help families stay together, remain independent, and cope with the pressures of modern life. A cornerstone of our efforts must be assisting families to support themselves. As Franklin Roosevelt said almost thirty years ago, "Self-help and self-control are the essence of the American tradition."

In Washington everyone looks out for special interest groups. Well, I think families are pretty special. And with your help, we'll continue looking out for their interests.

-Radio address, December 3, 1983

True Love Waits

Well, if I might interject a personal thought here, there's something I've always wanted to say to a group of young people like all of you. Yes, you get a lot of advice from those of us who are older. But I feel so deeply about what I'm about to say that, well, I'm going to go right ahead and give you one more piece of advice.

I'm sure that each of you believes that someday you'll find someone to fall in love with, and you will. And sometimes you may get frustrated, and, yes, finding the right one may take longer than you thought. But don't worry, it will happen. For each of you, out there someplace is that man or woman. And it's important for you not to pay any attention at all to all those who say that promiscuity is somehow stylish or rewarding. You know that when you meet that person, and meet them in marriage, that you will be true to each other. Well, did you ever stop to think you can start being true to that one special person beginning now?

-Remarks to the Student Congress
on Evangelism, July 28, 1988

The Spirit of the Family

As president I've often talked of the need to reaffirm the faith and the principles that made America great, and the family is basic to our nation's inner spirit. The family is our school of conscience, of service, of democracy, of love, of all things that we as a people esteem and treasure. Our basic values determine how well our republic holds together, whether it transmits to new generations sources of its inspiration and strength.

Someone once said there are only two lasting bequests that we can hope to give our children. One of them is roots, and the other is wings. Well, the family can help to provide both—the security of roots, the inspiration of wings. And this administration has tried hard to encourage both.

Our goals are plain. Where families are threatened, we seek to lessen those threats. Where families lack opportunities, we seek to provide them. And as Thanksgiving nears and we count our blessings, the family should be held chief among them.

-Remarks on signing the National Family Week
Proclamation, November 12, 1982

7 | SPIRITUAL RENEWAL AND REVIVAL

> Perhaps it's not too much to hope that true change will come to all countries that now deny or hinder the freedom to worship God. And perhaps we'll see that change comes through the reemergence of faith, through the irresistible power of a religious renewal. – 1987

Restoring America's Spiritual Roots

Well, I'm not going to preach a sermon. I thought instead I'd simply share a few thoughts with you on a subject I've had the opportunity to think about quite a bit during the years I've held this office: the subject of moral and religious values in our public life. And first I'd like to spend a moment or two looking at the history of religion in our public life, and then I'd like to speak about the challenge before us today.

Whenever I consider the history of this nation, I'm struck by how deeply imbued with faith the American people were, even from the very first. Many of the first settlers came for the express purpose of worshiping in freedom. Historian Samuel Morison wrote of one such group: "Doubting nothing and fearing no man, they undertook all to set all crooked ways straight and create a new Heaven and a new Earth. If they were not permitted to do that in England, they would find some other place to establish their city of God." Well, that place was this broad and open land we call America.

The debates over independence and the records of the Constitutional Convention make it clear that the Founding Fathers were sustained by their faith in God. In the Declaration of Independence itself, Thomas Jefferson wrote all men are "endowed by their Creator with certain inalienable rights." And it was George Washington who said, "Of all the dispositions and habits which lead to political prosperity, religion and morality are indispensable supports." Well, later, the statesmen gathered in Philadelphia to write what would become our Constitution. They often found themselves at odds, their purpose lost in acrimony and self-interest, until Benjamin Franklin stood one day and said, "I have been driven many times"—oh, no, I'm sorry—"I have lived a long time, and the longer I live, the more convincing proofs I see of this truth: that God governs in the affairs of men. And if a sparrow cannot fall to the ground without His notice, is it probable that an empire can rise without His aid?" And then he called that Constitutional Convention to open each day with prayer, which it did.

For decades, America remained a deeply religious country, thanking God in peacetime and turning to him in moments of crisis. During the Civil War, perhaps our nation's darkest hour, Abraham Lincoln said, "I have been driven many times to my knees by the conviction that I have nowhere else to go." Well, believe me, no one can serve in this office without understanding and believing exactly what he said....

And so it has been through most of our history. All our

material wealth and all our influence have been built on our faith in God and the bedrock values that follow from that faith. The great French philosopher visited our country—Alexis de Tocqueville—150 years ago. He wanted to see if he could find the secret of our greatness already, as a young country. And then he observed that "America is great because America is good. And if she ever ceases to be good, she will cease to be great." ...

You know, I know in our land of freedom everyone—if they want to choose atheism instead of a belief in God, that's their right to do so. But I have always felt that I would like someday to entertain an atheist at dinner and serve the most gourmet, perfect dinner that has ever been served and then, at the end of the meal, ask that atheist if he believes there's a cook. We must cherish our nation, work to make her better still, and never stop saying this simple prayer: God bless America.

Permit me to close now on a personal note with a few thoughts from my heart. You know, hardly a day goes by that I'm not told—sometimes in letters, sometimes by people I meet—that they're praying for me. It's a warm but humbling feeling. I know that many of you pray probably for me and for all our government leaders. Well, I appreciate your prayers more deeply than I can say. I grew up in a home where I was taught to believe in intercessory prayer. I know it's those prayers and millions like them that are building high and strong the cathedral of freedom that we call America, those prayers and millions like them that will always keep our country secure and make her a force for good in this too-troubled world. And that's why as a nation we must embrace our faith, for as long as we endeavor to do good—and we must believe that will be always—we will find our strength, our hope, and our true happiness in prayer and in the Lord's will.

-Remarks to the Student Congress
on Evangelism, July 28, 1988

---

*Pope John Paul II and
the Power of Religious Revival*

In your travels, you've inspired millions, people of all races and all faiths, who have felt the intensity of your desire for peace and brotherhood among men. As you embark on a pastoral visit to the land of your birth, Poland, be assured that the hearts of the American people are with you. Our prayers will go with you in profound hope that soon the hand of God will lighten the terrible burden of brave people everywhere who yearn for freedom, even as all men and women yearn for the freedom that God gave us all when he gave us a free will. We see the power of the spiritual force in that troubled land, uniting a people in hope, just as we see the powerful stirrings to the East of a belief that will not die despite generations of oppression. Perhaps it's not too much to hope that true change will come to all countries that now deny or hinder the freedom to worship God. And perhaps we'll see that change comes through the reemergence of faith, through the irresistible power of a religious renewal. For despite all the attempts to extinguish it, the people's faith burns with a passionate heat; once allowed to breathe free, that faith will burn so brightly it will light the world.

-Remarks following discussions with Pope John Paul II
in Vatican City, June 6, 1987

America's Divine Providence

The next few days, and maybe weeks, will probably be dominated, in terms of the news, by talk of economic matters—budgets and the tax structure and so forth. But I want you to know that as we begin the great work ahead of us, I've been thinking very much about Divine Providence and turning to our Lord and asking for His guidance. I have found myself, as Abraham Lincoln did once, driven to my knees more than ever because there was no place else to go.

But I'm also aware, as never before, that what the polls show is true: In virtually every public survey, there are indications that the importance of spiritual faith has grown stronger among the people of our country. Recent Gallup surveys show 64 percent of Americans—adults—express a great deal or quite a lot of confidence in the church of organized religion. Fifty-six percent of Americans believe that religion can answer all or most of today's problems. In fact, only one in five doubts the relevance of religion in the modern world. And we'll get them, too.

As a resident of 1600 Pennsylvania Avenue, I may have a special vantage point from which to judge these things. In December, when I looked north from the White House, I would see the huge menorah, celebrating the Passover [Hanukkah] season in Lafayette Park. And when I looked south from the Truman Balcony, I could see the Pageant of Peace and the crèche symbolizing the birth of Christ. Showing the symbols of our beliefs in this way and what it is, for many of us, the honest time of the year, is good—good for all of us, for Christians and Jews and any others who wish to share the joy of our holidays.

The other day I was at the National Prayer Breakfast here in Washington, and I spoke, as so many others did, of the central place of faith in our lives and how belief in something bigger than ourselves is probably a necessary precondition to peace. And I mentioned that after four years in this job, I know as never before that we are all God's children, that the clerk, the king, and, yes, the communist were made in His image.

And I've often wondered about one individual there, because when I said that, a fellow in the back of the room—I heard him say, "Amen." There were more than three thousand people in that room, from almost every country in the globe—African chiefs, Central American businessmen, people from Australia and Europe and the Middle East. And the room seemed to hum with agreement that faith and belief are the key to man's salvation and the only way we'll learn to live with each other in peace.

All of you are doing your part to fill the world with God's work and make more gentle man's life on Earth. Like St. Peter and his brother, St. Andrew, you've been good and faithful fishermen, and you've fought the good fight—for prayer in the schools and against abortion and for freedom in the world. You know, perhaps better than I, that you have never let us down.

And I'm not shy today about asking you for your continued support in many areas, including our economic program. It occurs to me that the doctrine of election means one thing to some of you and quite another to those of us who hold public office. When I was reelected in November, I didn't figure I was being sent back to the White House to turn back to the policies of the past. I still believe the government is the servant of the people and not the other way around.

We're trying to get government spending down, to hold

down the huge cost of government, to keep it from taking the money you deserve to keep for your family and your future and for God's work. We mean to ensure greater possibility for the production of wealth by lowering tax rates through tax reform. We mean to maintain a strong defense, because only with a strong defense can we preserve the peace we cherish.

And I found myself wanting to remind you of what Jesus said in Luke 14:31: "Oh, what king, when he sets out to meet another king in battle will not first sit down and take counsel whether he is strong enough with ten thousand men to encounter the one coming against him with twenty thousand. Or else, while the other is still far away, sends a delegation and asks the terms of peace." I don't think the Lord that blessed this country, as no other country has ever been blessed, intends for us to have to someday negotiate because of our weakness.

But all of these things I've mentioned are pretty revolutionary. All of these things—learning to control the government, limiting the amount of money it can take from us, protecting our country through a strong defense—all of these things revolve around one word, and that word is "freedom." And as Jefferson said, "The Lord who gave us life, the God who gave us life gave us liberty also."

That's what we stand for here and everywhere. And that's what I need your continued help in preserving and promoting. And every voice counts. These are crucial days ahead of us, in terms of the budget and taxes and keeping our commitment to rebuild our defenses.

I need all of you as never before. And we need Him as never before. And we mustn't doubt at all that He will give us help and support and encouragement and guidance. You've given me these things time and again. And for all of this, I am truly thankful.

-Remarks, Convention of the National
Religious Broadcasters, February 4, 1985

The Bible Contains All the Answers

Abraham Lincoln called the Bible "the best gift God has given to man." "But for it," he said, "we could not know right from wrong." Like that image of George Washington kneeling in prayer in the snow at Valley Forge, Lincoln described a people who knew it was not enough to depend on their own courage and goodness; they must also look to God their Father and Preserver. And their faith to walk with Him and trust in His Word brought them the blessings of comfort, power, and peace that they sought.

The torch of their faith has been passed from generation to generation. "The grass withereth, the flower fadeth, but the Word of our God shall stand forever" (see Is 40:8).

More and more Americans believe that loving God in their hearts is the ultimate value. Last year, not only were Year of the Bible activities held in every state of the Union, but more than twenty-five states and five hundred cities issued their own Year of the Bible proclamations. One schoolteacher, Mary Gibson, in New York raised $4,000 to buy Bibles for working people in downtown Manhattan.

Nineteen eighty-three was the year more of us read the Good Book. Can we make a resolution here today?—that 1984 will be the year we put its great truths into action?

My experience in this office I hold has only deepened a belief I've held for many years: Within the covers of that single Book are all the answers to all the problems that face us today if we'd only read and believe.

Let's begin at the beginning. God is the center of our lives; the human family stands at the center of society; and our greatest hope for the future is in the faces of our children. Seven thousand Poles recently came to the christening of Maria Victoria Walesa, daughter of Danuta and Lech Walesa, to express their belief that solidarity of the family remains the foundation of freedom.

God's most blessed gift to His family is the gift of life. He sent us the Prince of Peace as a babe in a manger. I've said that we must be cautious in claiming God is on our side. I think the real question we must answer is, are we on His side?

-Remarks, Annual Convention of the National
Religious Broadcasters, January 30, 1984

Living the Ten Commandments

How much money could we save, how much better off might Americans be if all of us tried a little harder to live by the Ten Commandments and the Golden Rule? I've been told that since the beginning of civilization millions and millions of laws have been written. I've even heard someone suggest it was as many as several billion. And yet, taken all together, all those millions and millions of laws have not improved on the Ten Commandments one bit.

-Remarks, Annual Convention of the National
Religious Broadcasters, January 30, 1984

Hungry for Spiritual Revival

As a nation, we're struggling to guide ourselves safely through stormy seas. We need all the help we can get. I think the American people are hungry for spiritual revival. More and more of us are beginning to sense that we can't have it both ways. We can't just expect God to protect us in a crisis and just leave him over there on the shelf in our day-to-day living. I wonder if sometimes he isn't waiting for us to wake up and that he isn't maybe running out of patience.

-Remarks at Kansas State University,
September 9, 1982

8 | THE CONSCIENCE OF A NATION

> I'm only the head of a civil government,
> a secular authority. It's probably true that
> politics is the prose of a culture, but religion
> is its poetry. Governments are passing things
> in the long history of the world, but faith
> and belief endure forever. – 1984

Faith Is the Prerequisite to Freedom

Our own experience on this continent—the American experience—though brief, has had one unmistakable encounter, an insistence on the preservation of one sacred truth. It is a truth that our first president, our Founding Father, passed on in the first farewell address made to the American people. It is a truth that I hope now you'll permit me to mention in these remarks of farewell, a truth embodied in our Declaration of Independence: that the case for inalienable rights, that the idea of human dignity, that the notion of conscience above compulsion can be made only in the context of higher law, only in the context of what one of the founders of this organization [the United Nations], Secretary-General Dag Hammarskjöld, has called devotion to something which is greater and higher than we are ourselves. This is the endless cycle, the final truth to which humankind seems always to return: that religion and morality, that faith in something higher, are prerequisites for freedom, and that justice and peace within ourselves is the first step toward justice and peace in the world and for the ages.

Yes, this is a place of great debate and grave discussions. And yet I cannot help but note here that one of our Founding Fathers, the most worldly of men, an internationalist, Benjamin Franklin, interrupted the proceedings of our own Constitutional Convention to make much the same point. And I cannot help but think this morning of other beginnings, of where and when I first read those words: "And they shall beat their swords into plowshares ..." and "your young men shall see visions and your old men shall dream dreams...." This morning, my thoughts go to her who gave me many things in life, but her most important gift was the knowledge of happiness and solace to be gained in prayer. It's the greatest help I've had in my presidency, and I recall here Lincoln's words when he said only the most foolish of men would think he could confront the duties of the office I now hold without turning to someone stronger, a power above all others.

I think then of her and others like her in that small town in Illinois, gentle people who possessed something that those who hold positions of power sometimes forget to prize. No one of them could ever have imagined the boy from the banks of the Rock River would come to this moment and have this opportunity. But had they been told it would happen, I think they would have been a bit disappointed if I'd not spoken here for what they knew so well: that when we grow weary of the world and its troubles, when our faith in humanity falters, it is then that we must seek comfort and refreshment of spirit in a deeper source of wisdom, one greater than ourselves.

And so, if future generations do say of us that in our time peace came closer, that we did bring about new seasons of truth and justice, it will be cause for pride. But it shall be a cause of greater pride, still, if it is also said that we were wise enough to know the deliberations of great leaders and great bodies are but an overture, that the truly majestic music—the music of freedom, of justice, and peace—is the music made in forgetting self and seeking in silence the will of Him who made us.

-Address to the 43rd Session of the
United Nations General Assembly in
New York, New York, September 26, 1988

God Is the Foundation of Democracy

The faith in the dignity of the individual under God is the foundation for the whole American political experiment. It is central to our national politics. Our first president put it all very well. He said, "Of all the dispositions and habits which lead to political prosperity, religion and morality are indispensable supports." And, incidentally, to those who suggest that the two could be separated, he further pointed out that morality could not really be sustained or widely observed without religion. There can be no freedom without order, and there can be no order without virtue. Now, that's a simple enough formulation, but it's an insight found not only in the writings of Founding Fathers like Washington or great political thinkers like Edmund Burke; it is also found in a great part of our Judeo-Christian tradition—notably in the modern encyclicals of Popes Leo XII and

John Paul II. Yet how often this simple truth, the importance of this belief in basic values, is overlooked in a society of high technology and mass communication and bewildering, everyday events. I guess what I'm trying to say was put very well by the great Catholic essayist G.K. Chesterton when he warned about the modern habit of those who try to put the heavens in their heads rather than their heads in the heavens. Or as Alfred North Whitehead observed, "There is a danger in clarity, the danger of overlooking the subtleties of truth." Those subtleties of truth—the belief in the importance of family, of community, and church—the realization that the Western idea of freedom and democracy spring directly from Judeo-Christian religious experience are not often publicly discussed. Yet these are the things that still remain the foundation for our concepts of social justice, our political system, our very way of life. They are the values that ennoble man, making him something more that just the plaything of hedonism or the vassal of dictatorship; they entitle him to personal dignity and to the individual liberty and representative government that dignity enjoins.

- Remarks to the Supreme Council of the Knights of
Columbus, Hartford, Connecticut, August 3, 1982

The Principles of Religious Liberty

America's creed of liberty has never been expressed better than in the words of the Book of Leviticus emblazoned on the Liberty Bell, "Proclaim liberty throughout all the land unto all the inhabitants thereof." The American people have long recognized that the liberty we cherish must include the freedom to worship God as each of us pleases. We can all rejoice in noting that a critical step in the history of this freedom was taken nearly two centuries ago this month.

On September 25, 1789, the Congress proposed and sent to the states for ratification a series of ten amendments to the new Constitution. This Bill of Rights would safeguard and perpetuate the rights and liberties for which the American people had fought the War of Independence and the states had ratified the Constitution. Because of the First Amendment's vital clauses— "Congress shall make no law respecting an establishment of religion, or prohibiting the free exercise thereof;..."—the 199th anniversary of the introduction of the Bill of Rights is a fitting time to begin a week in celebration of religious freedom.

The religious liberty described in this amendment is the protection of religion and conscience from government interference. It creates neither hostility between government and religion nor a civil religion of secularism. The fundamental principle of religious liberty, that government can neither forbid nor force the people's practice of religion, was essential to the founding of our nation. Our leaders knew that faith blesses men and nations alike as it fosters morality and justice. George Washington stated in his farewell address, "Reason and experience both forbid us to expect that national morality can prevail in exclusion of religious principle." The Northwest Ordinance of 1787, which the Congress reenacted in 1789, similarly stated, "Religion, morality, and knowledge being necessary to good government and the happiness of mankind, schools and the means of learning shall forever be encouraged."

The Founders realized that we must guard freedom of religion with eternal vigilance against tyranny and bigotry.

Washington emphasized this in a letter to Moses Seixas of the Hebrew Congregation of Touro Synagogue in Newport, Rhode Island, in 1790. Our first president noted Americans' "liberty of conscience and immunities of citizenship" and said that it was not "by the indulgence of one class of their inherent natural rights." Rather, "happily the Government of the United States,... gives to bigotry no sanction, to persecution no assistance...."

President Washington proudly called this policy "enlarged and liberal" and "worthy of imitation." Through the years, Americans of goodwill have echoed these sentiments, seeking freedom, brotherhood, justice, and reconciliation. We will always do so if we continue to revere the First Amendment's protection of religious freedom.

-A proclamation, Religious Freedom Week,
September 27, 1988

One Nation Under God

We are a nation under God. I've always believed that this blessed land was set apart in a special way, that some divine plan placed this great continent here between the oceans to be found by people from every corner of the Earth who had a special love for freedom and the courage to uproot themselves, leave homeland and friends, to come to a strange land. And coming here they created something new in all the history of mankind—a land where man is not beholden to government, government is beholden to man. George Washington believed that religion, morality, and brotherhood were the pillars of society. He said you couldn't have morality without religion. And yet today we're told that to protect the First Amendment, we must expel God, the source of all knowledge, from our children's classrooms. Well, pardon me, but the First Amendment was not written to protect American people from religion; the first amendment was written to protect the American people from government tyranny.

-Remarks at a Spirit of America Rally,
Atlanta, Georgia, January 26, 1984

Touching the Face of God

Ladies and gentlemen, I'd planned to speak to you tonight to report on the state of the union, but the events of earlier today have led me to change those plans. Today is a day for mourning and remembering. Nancy and I are pained to the core by the tragedy of the shuttle Challenger. We know we share this pain with all of the people of our country. This is truly a national loss.

Nineteen years ago, almost to the day, we lost three astronauts in a terrible accident on the ground. But we've never lost an astronaut in flight; we've never had a tragedy like this. And perhaps we've forgotten the courage it took for the crew of the shuttle. But they, the Challenger Seven, were aware of the dangers, overcame them, and did their jobs brilliantly. We mourn seven heroes: Michael Smith, Dick Scobee, Judith Resnik, Ronald McNair, Ellison Onizuka, Gregory Jarvis, and Christa McAuliffe. We mourn their loss as a nation together.

[To] the families of the seven: we cannot bear, as you do, the full impact of this tragedy. But we feel the loss, and we're thinking about you so very much. Your loved ones were daring and brave, and they had that special grace, that special spirit that says, "Give me a challenge, and I'll meet it with joy." They had a hunger to explore the universe and discover its truths. They wished to serve, and they did. They served all of us. We've grown used to wonders in this century. It's hard to dazzle us. But for twenty-five years the United States space program has been doing just that. We've grown used to the idea of space, and perhaps we forget that we've only just begun. We're still pioneers. They, the members of the Challenger crew, were pioneers.

And I want to say something to the schoolchildren of America who were watching the live coverage of the shuttle's takeoff. I know it is hard to understand, but sometimes painful things like this happen. It's all part of the process of exploration and discovery. It's all part of taking a chance and expanding man's horizons. The future doesn't belong to the fainthearted; it belongs to the brave. The Challenger crew was pulling us into the future, and we'll continue to follow them.

I've always had great faith in and respect for our space program, and what happened today does nothing to diminish it. We don't hide our space program. We don't keep secrets and cover things up. We do it all up front and in public. That's the way freedom is, and we wouldn't change it for a minute. We'll continue our quest in space. There will be more shuttle flights and more shuttle crews and, yes, more volunteers, more civilians, more teachers in space. Nothing ends here; our hopes and our journeys continue. I want to add that I wish I could talk to every man and woman who works for NASA or who worked on this mission and tell them: "Your dedication and professionalism have moved and impressed us for decades. And we know of your anguish. We share it."

There's a coincidence today. On this day 390 years ago, the great explorer Sir Francis Drake died aboard ship off the coast of Panama. In his lifetime the great frontiers were the oceans, and a historian later said, "He lived by the sea, died on it, and was buried in it." Well, today we can say of the Challenger crew: Their dedication was, like Drake's, complete.

The crew of the space shuttle Challenger honored us by the manner in which they lived their lives. We will never forget them, nor the last time we saw them, this morning, as they prepared for their journey and waved goodbye and "slipped the surly bonds of earth" to "touch the face of God."

Thank you.

-Televised address, January 26, 1986
(Space Shuttle Challenger)

Religion Is the Conscience of Democracy

There was reason to imagine that the American experiment could not last; and that there were moments when men of good will thought the experiment was doomed, as during those tragic Civil War years, when American fought against American and tore this country asunder so that it could be reassembled as a freer and better place. There have been other experiments as well during these centuries—terrible, awful experiments that demonstrate just how unyielding is God's commitment to the covenant he made with Abraham. For there must have been times, in the showers of Treblinka or on the killing fields of Cambodia or in the forests of Katyn, when men and women in their anguish and despair must have expected that the Great Flood would once again sweep away the sinning nations. Or they might have been seized with the same sentiment as the poet Yeats when haunted by the sight of a world in which "the best lack all conviction, while the worst are full of passionate intensity." "Surely," Yeats wrote, "some revolution—revelation," I should say, "is at hand; surely the Second Coming is at hand."

Well, yesterday we commemorated a dark day in the course of our century: the fiftieth anniversary of the signing of the Munich pact. On this day fifty years ago, Prime Minister Neville Chamberlain returned to Britain and proclaimed that he had brought "peace in our time." And eleven months later, Nazi Germany invaded Poland, hurling that nation into a nightmare from which it has yet to awaken and throwing the world into war. And yet, just at the very moments that the worst seemed destined to defeat the best, the best pulled something out of themselves and were not consumed. Three barbaric governments were eliminated, and Germany, Italy, and Japan became inseparable allies to those whom they had fought only a few years before.

And though millions and millions still live under the yoke of communism, they have proved that the human spirit cannot be consumed either. There have been men and women who make us gasp with wonder at the greatness thrust upon them when oppression proved too much to tolerate. I think of the sight of Natan Shcharanskiy still in the dominion of his KGB captors, zigzagging his way across the tarmac after they ordered him to walk a straight line from the plane that had carried him to freedom. It was one of those moments when laughter and tears commingle, and one does not know when the first leaves off and the second begins. It was a vision of the purest freedom known to man, the freedom of a man whose cause is just and whose faith is his guiding light.

At its full flowering, freedom is the first principle of society; this society, Western society. Indeed, from Abraham to Plato, Aristotle to Aquinas, freedom is the animating principle of Western civilization. Freedom comes in many guises: in the noble words of the Declaration of Independence and in the noble souls of people like Shcharanskiy. And yet freedom cannot exist alone. And that's why the theme for your bicentennial is so very apt: learning, faith, and freedom. Each reinforces the others, each makes the others possible. For what are they without each other?

Learning is a good thing, but unless it's tempered by faith and a love of freedom, it can be very dangerous indeed. The names of many intellectuals are recorded on the rolls of infamy, from Robespierre to Lenin to Ho Chi Minh to Pol Pot. We must never forget that wisdom is impossible without learning, but learning does not—not by the longest measure—bring wisdom. It can also bring evil. What will faith without a respect for learning and an understanding of freedom bring? We've seen the tragedy of untempered faith in the hellish deaths of fourteen-year-old boys—small hands still wrapped around machine guns, on the front lines in Iran.

And what will be wrought by freedom unaccompanied by learning and faith?—the license of Weimar Germany and the decadence of imperial Rome; human behavior untempered by a sense of moral, spiritual, or intellectual limits—the behavior G.K. Chesterton described as the "morbid weakness of always sacrificing the normal to the abnormal." And when freedom is mangled in this way, what George Orwell would have called unfreedom soon follows.

So, we like to believe, and we pray it will always be so, that America is different, that America is what she is because she is guided by all three: learning, faith, and freedom. Our love of knowledge has made this nation the intellectual and technological center of the world. Our commitment to protecting and preserving the freedoms we enjoy is unshakable. And our faith is what supports us. Tocqueville said it in 1835, and it's as true today as it was then: "Despotism may govern without faith, but liberty cannot. Religion is more needed in democratic societies than in any others."

Americans know the truth of those words. We still believe in our Creator. We still believe in knowledge. We still believe in freedom. We're committed to providing the world with the bounties we enjoy, and we're sickened by those societies that do dishonor to humankind by denying human beings their birthright. We grieve for the millions who have perished even in this decade because their freedoms were denied, and we must not dishonor them by allowing those who follow us on this Earth to say those millions died for nothing, that we lived in an age of barbarism.

No, ladies and gentlemen, I believe that if we hold fast and true to our principles our time will come to be known as the age of freedom. There are signs—and they're only signs—that suggest the rulers who enslave and victimize the people of the Earth are on the ideological defensive. Their claims for the superiority of failed and terrible philosophies are sounding ever more hollow. The societies they designed to be utopias have not, to put it mildly, turned out as planned. To save themselves, those rulers are beginning to cast their eyes toward the democratic societies they used to revile. There are signs, only signs, that these rulers are beginning to understand the secret to our prosperity: We prosper economically only because people are free, free not only to speak and read and think but also to create and build and barter and sell.

Now, we're fast approaching a turning point in the history of this age. It'll determine whether history will deem our time the age of freedom or the age of barbarism. We have been steadfast and unapologetic about our defense of our beliefs and our defense of our societies. We learned the lesson of Munich. When we were told that the time had come to accept Soviet nuclear superiority in Europe, we said we would never accept it; when we were told that the time had come to accept the Soviet dominion over Afghanistan, we said we would never accept it; and when we were told that we had no chance to dislodge Soviet proxies in Angola and Nicaragua, we said we would never accept it.

And you all now know what has happened. In the last eight years, not an inch of ground has fallen to communism. Indeed, we liberated the island of Grenada from the "mere anarchy" it had fallen into under communist rule, and set it on the road to democracy. And we helped save a country from communism and watched it flower into a democracy in the midst of a civil war: the nation of El Salvador. Yes, at every point on the map that the Soviets have applied pressure, we've done all we can to apply pressure against them. And now we're seeing a sight many believed they would never see in our lifetime: the receding of the tide of totalitarianism.

-Remarks at Georgetown University's
Bicentennial Convocation, October 1, 1988

A Spiritual Awakening

America has begun a spiritual awakening. Faith and hope are being restored. Americans are turning back to God. Church attendance is up. Audiences for religious books and broadcasts are growing. On college campuses, students have stopped shunning religion and started going to church. As Harvard theologian Harvey Cox put it—and I quote—"Rather than the cynical, careerist types who supposedly have filled the campuses, I see young people who are intensely interested in moral issues, in religious history and beliefs."

One of my favorite Bible quotations comes from Second Chronicles: "If My people who are called by My name humble themselves and pray and seek My face, and turn from their wicked ways, then will I hear from heaven, and forgive their sin and heal their land" (see 2 Chr 7:14). Today Americans from Maine to California are seeking His face. And I do believe that He has begun to heal our blessed land.

As this special awakening gathers strength, we must remember that many in good faith will hold other views. Let us pledge to conduct ourselves with generosity, tolerance, and openness toward all. We must respect the rights and views of every American, because we're unshakably committed to democratic values. Our Maker would have it no less.

So, please use your pulpits to denounce racism, anti-Semitism, and all ethnic or religious intolerance as evils, and let us make it clear that our values must not restrict, but liberate the human spirit in thought and in deed.

You may remember, but I'm sure you don't agree with, a very cynical quote that got wide circulation, from H.L. Mencken. He said Puritanism "is the haunting fear that someone, somewhere, may be happy." Well, some suspect that today's spiritual awakening reflects such narrow-mindedness. We must show that faith and traditional values are the things that give life human dignity, warmth, vitality, and yes, laughter and joy....

In this age when electronics beam messages around the globe, we must keep telling the truth, including the truth about the difference between free and totalitarian societies.

This month it will be my honor to award a posthumous Medal of Honor—a Medal of Freedom, I should say—to Whittaker Chambers, a man of courage and wisdom. Chambers understood the struggle between totalitarianism and the West. He, himself, had turned to communism out of a sense of idealism in which he thought that might be the answer. And then he wrote, all the great visions of the free world "have always been different versions of the same vision: the vision of God and man's relationship to God. The communist vision is the vision of man without God."

I don't know whether you've ever read his line of when he first began to awaken. They had a new baby, a little girl. And he was looking at her one morning as she sat in her highchair. And he said he found himself looking at the delicate convolutions of that tiny ear. And that was when he said to himself, "That cannot be just an accident of nature, a freak of nature." And he said he may not have realized it at the moment, but he knows that in that moment, God had laid His finger on his forehead.

When men try to live in a world without God, it's only too easy for them to forget the rights that God bestows—too easy to suppress freedom of speech, to build walls to keep their countrymen in, to jail dissidents, and to put great thinkers in mental wards. We will deal with the communist world as we must with a great power: by negotiating with it, from strength and in good faith.

And if the new Soviet leadership is willing, we will renew our efforts to ease tensions between East and West. And while we will never accept for ourselves their system, we will never stop praying that the leaders, like so many of their own people, might come to know the liberating nature of faith in God....

Saint Paul wrote a verse that I've always cherished: "Now abide faith, hope, love, these three; but the greatest of these is love" (see 1 Cor 13:13). May we have faith in our God and in all the good that we can do with His help. May we stand firm in the hope of making America all that she can be—a nation of opportunity and prosperity and a force for peace and goodwill among nations. And may we remain steadfast in our love for this green and gentle land and the freedom that she offers.

-Remarks at the annual convention of the
National Association of Evangelicals,
Columbus, Ohio, March 6, 1984

Standing Up for God

Standing up for America also means standing up for God who has so blessed this land. If we could just keep remembering that Moses brought down from the mountain the Ten Commandments, not ten suggestions—and if one of us who lived for the Lord could remember that He wants us to love our Lord and our neighbor, then there's no limit to the problems we could solve or the mountains we could climb together as a mighty force for good. The United States remains the last, best hope for mankind plagued by tyranny and deprivation. America is no stronger than its people—and that means you and me. Well, I believe in you, and I believe that if we work together, then one day we will say, "We fought the good fight. We finished the race. We kept the faith." And to our children's children we can say, "We did all that could be done in the brief time that was given us here on Earth."

-Remarks to the National Rifle Association,
Phoenix, Arizona, May 6, 1983

Religion and Culture

I'm only the head of a civil government, a secular authority. It's probably true that politics is the prose of a culture, but religion is its poetry. Governments are passing things in the long history of the world, but faith and belief endure forever.

-Remarks at the St. Ann's Festival in
Hoboken, New Jersey, July 26, 1984

Morality in Public Policy

I believe that politics and religion are related, because I do not believe you can function in politics without some sense of morality. It is through our religious beliefs that our moral tradition in the West is descended. While a legislator or a president may not bring to his politics the specific tenets of his particular faith, each of us brings a code of morals to bear on our judgments. There is much talk in this country now of religions interfering with politics. Actually, it is the other way around. Politics—legalization of abortion; attempts to fund abortion with taxpayers' money; prohibition of voluntary prayer in public schools; weakening of laws against pornography; failure to enforce civil rights legislation on behalf of helpless, severely ill infants—has moved across the barrier between church and state and the arena of religious beliefs. Most of Western civilization is based on the Judeo-Christian ethic. The wall of separation between church and state in America was erected by our forefathers to protect religion from the state, not the other way around.

-White House press conference,
November 3, 1984

9 | THE BIBLE AND CULTURE

> When Americans reach out for values of
> faith, family, and caring for the needy, they're
> saying, "We want the Word of God. We want
> to face the future with the Bible." – 1984

Seeking the Face of God

The Bible says: "If my people who are called by my name humble themselves and pray and seek my face and turn from their wicked ways, then I will hear from heaven and forgive their sins and heal their land" (see 2 Chr 7:14). Many, many years ago, my mother had underlined that particular passage in the Bible. And I had her Bible that I could place my hand on when I took the oath of office in 1980. And I had it opened to that passage that she had underlined. Today more and more Americans are seeking His face. And, yes, He has begun to heal our land.

-Remarks to the Student Congress on
Evangelism, July 28, 1988

The Bible and the Constitition

Isaiah reminded us that "the Lord opens His gates and keeps in peace the nation that trusts in Him." I hope you won't mind my saying I think I know you all very well. Nelle Reagan, my mother, God rest her soul, had an unshakable faith in God's goodness. And while I may not have realized it in my youth, I know now that she planted that faith very deeply in me. She made the most difficult Christian message seem very easy. And, like you, she knew you could never repay one bad deed with another. Her way was forgiveness and goodness, and both began with love.

For some time now I believe that America has been hungering for a return to spiritual values that some of us fear we've tended to forget—things like faith, families, family values, the bedrock of our nation. Thanks to the creation of new networks of faith by so many of you and your families, we're seeing more clearly again. We're remembering that freedom carries responsibilities. And we're not set free so that we can become slaves to sin.

The Founding Fathers believed that faith in God was the key to our being a good people and America's becoming a great nation. George Washington kissed the Bible at his inauguration. And to those who would have government separate us from religion, he had these words: "Reason and experience both forbid us to expect that national morality can prevail in exclusion of religious principle." And Ben Franklin, at the time when they were struggling with what was to be the American Constitution, finally one day said to those who were working with him that, "Without God's help, we shall succeed in this political building no better than the builders of Babel." And if we ever forget that, we're lost. From that day on they opened all of the constitutional meetings with prayer.

I pray that we don't lose that idea, and that's why I was motivated to proclaim or designate 1983 the Year of the Bible.

And I hope that we will also recognize the true meaning of the First Amendment. Its words were meant to guarantee freedom of religion to everyone. But I believe the First Amendment has been twisted to the point that freedom of religion is in danger of becoming freedom from religion. But keep the faith. This year the Supreme Court took two big steps toward common sense. It said that the First Amendment does not prevent legislators in the Nebraska State Assembly from hiring a chaplain to open their sessions with prayer. And it said the Constitution does not prevent the state of Minnesota from giving a tax break to parents who choose private or religious schooling for their children. In both cases the Court decided in favor of what our Justice Department recommended in friend-of-the-court briefs.

Now we're making another recommendation. We believe the city of Pawtucket, Rhode Island, and for that matter, any city in America, has the right to include the nativity scene as part of its annual Christmas performance.

Government is not supposed to wage war against God and religion, not in the United States of America. I want to see the Congress act on our constitutional amendment permitting voluntary prayer in America's schoolrooms. And here you can be our greatest help. Tell the millions of our friends to send a message of thunder from the grassroots, fill the halls of Congress with calls, with letters and telegrams—not postcards. I understand they don't take postcards as seriously as they take letters.

And tell them, "The people have waited too long; we want action."

-Remarks to leaders of Christian religious
organizations, October 13, 1983

America Needs the Bible

I don't speak as a theologian or a scholar, only as one who's lived a little more than his threescore ten—which has been a source of annoyance to some—and as one who has been active in the political life of the nation for roughly four decades and now who's served the past three and one-half years in our highest office. I speak, I think I can say, as one who has seen much, who has loved his country, and who's seen it change in many ways.

I believe that faith and religion play a critical role in the political life of our nation—and always have—and that the church—and by that I mean all churches, all denominations—has had a strong influence on the state. And this has worked to our benefit as a nation.

Those who created our country—the Founding Fathers and Mothers—understood that there is a divine order which transcends the human order. They saw the state, in fact, as a form of moral order and felt that the bedrock of moral order is religion.

The Mayflower Compact began with the words, "In the name of God, amen." The Declaration of Independence appeals to "Nature's God" and the "Creator" and the "Supreme Judge of the world." Congress was given a chaplain, and the oaths of office are oaths before God.

James Madison, in the Federalist papers, admitted that in the creation of our republic he perceived the hand of the Almighty. John Jay, the first chief justice of the Supreme Court, warned that we must never forget the God from whom our blessings flow.

Religion played not only a strong role in our national life; it played a positive role. The abolitionist movement was at heart a moral and religious movement; so was the modern civil rights struggle. And throughout this time, the state was tolerant of religious belief, expression, and practice. Society, too, was tolerant.

But in the 1960s this began to change. We began to make great steps toward secularizing our nation and removing religion from its honored place.

In 1962 the Supreme Court in the New York prayer case banned the compulsory saying of prayers. In 1963 the Court banned the reading of the Bible in our public schools. From that point on, the courts pushed the meaning of the ruling ever outward, so that now our children are not allowed voluntary prayer. We even had to pass a law—we passed a special law in the Congress just a few weeks ago to allow student prayer groups the same access to schoolrooms after classes that a young Marxist society, for example, would already enjoy with no opposition.

The 1962 decision opened the way to a flood of similar suits. Once religion had been made vulnerable, a series of assaults were made in one court after another, on one issue after another. Cases were started to argue against tax-exempt-status churches. Suits were brought to abolish the words "under

God" from the Pledge of Allegiance and to remove "In God We Trust" from public documents and from our currency.

Today there are those who are fighting to make sure voluntary prayer is not returned to the classrooms. And the frustrating thing for the great majority of Americans who support and understand the special importance of religion in the national life—the frustrating thing is that those who are attacking religion claim they are doing it in the name of tolerance, freedom, and open-mindedness. Question: Isn't the real truth that they are intolerant of religion? They refuse to tolerate its importance in our lives.

If all the children of our country studied together all of the many religions in our country, wouldn't they learn greater tolerance of each other's beliefs? If children prayed together, would they not understand what they have in common, and would this not, indeed, bring them closer, and is this not to be desired? So, I submit to you that those who claim to be fighting for tolerance on this issue may not be tolerant at all.

When John Kennedy was running for president in 1960, he said that his church would not dictate his presidency any more than he would speak for his church. Just so, and proper. But John Kennedy was speaking in an America in which the role of religion—and by that I mean the role of all churches—was secure. Abortion was not a political issue. Prayer was not a political issue. The right of church schools to operate was not a political issue. And it was broadly acknowledged that religious leaders had a right and a duty to speak out on the issues of the day. They held a place of respect, and a politician who spoke to or of them with a lack of respect would not long survive in the political arena.

It was acknowledged then that religion held a special place, occupied a special territory in the hearts of the citizenry. The climate has changed greatly since then. And since it has, it logically follows that religion needs defenders against those who care only for the interests of the state.

There are, these days, many questions on which religious leaders are obliged to offer their moral and theological guidance, and such guidance is a good and necessary thing. To know how a church and its members feel on a public issue expands the parameters of debate. It does not narrow the debate; it expands it.

The truth is, politics and morality are inseparable. And as morality's foundation is religion, religion and politics are necessarily related. We need religion as a guide. We need it because we are imperfect, and our government needs the church, because only those humble enough to admit they're sinners can bring to democracy the tolerance it requires in order to survive.

A state is nothing more than a reflection of its citizens; the more decent the citizens, the more decent the state. If you practice a religion, whether you're Catholic, Protestant, Jewish, or guided by some other faith, then your private life will be influenced by a sense of moral obligation, and so, too, will your public life. One affects the other. The churches of America do not exist by the grace of the state; the churches of America are not mere citizens of the state. The churches of America exist apart; they have their own vantage point, their own authority. Religion is its own realm; it makes its own claims.

We establish no religion in this country, nor will we ever. We command no worship. We mandate no belief. But we poison our society when we remove its theological underpinnings. We court corruption when we leave it bereft of belief. All are free to believe or not believe; all are free to practice a faith or not. But those who believe must be free to speak of and act on their belief, to apply moral teaching to public questions.

I submit to you that the tolerant society is open to and encouraging of all religions. And this does not weaken us; it strengthens us, it makes us strong. You know, if we look back through history to all those great civilizations, those great nations that rose up to even world dominance and then deteriorated, declined, and fell, we find they all had one thing in common. One of the significant forerunners of their fall was their turning away from their God or gods.

Without God, there is no virtue, because there's no prompting of the conscience. Without God, we're mired in the material, that flat world that tells us only what the senses perceive. Without God, there is a coarsening of the society. And without God, democracy will not and cannot long endure. If we ever forget that we're one nation under God, then we will be a nation gone under.

If I could just make a personal statement of my own—in these three and one-half years I have understood and known better than ever before the words of Lincoln, when he said that he would be the greatest fool on this footstool called Earth if he ever thought that for one moment he could perform the duties of that office without help from One who is stronger than all.

-Remarks at an ecumenical prayer breakfast,
Dallas, Texas, August 23, 1984

The Wisdom of God's Word

I'm so thankful that there will always be one day in the year when people all over our land can sit down as neighbors and friends and remind ourselves of what our real task is. This task was spelled out in the Old and the New Testament. Jesus was asked, "Master, which is the great commandment in the law?" And He replied, "Thou shalt love the Lord thy God with all thy heart, and with all thy soul, and with all thy mind. This is the first and great commandment. The second is like unto it, thou shalt love thy neighbour as thyself. On these two command-ments hang all the law and the prophets" (see Mt 22:36-40).

Can we resolve to reach, learn, and try to heed the greatest message ever written—God's Word and the Holy Bible? Inside its pages lie all the answers to all the problems that man has ever known....

When we think how many people in the world are impris-oned or tortured, harassed for even possessing a Bible or trying to read one, we might remember something that Abraham Lincoln said over a hundred years ago: "We have forgotten the gracious hand that preserved us in peace, and multiplied and enriched and strengthened us; and we have vainly imagined, in the deceitfulness of our hearts, that all these blessings were pro-duced by some superior wisdom and virtue of our own.... We have become too proud to pray to the God that made us!" Well, isn't it time for us to say, "We're not too proud to pray"?

We face great challenges in this country, but we've faced great challenges before and conquered them. What carried us through was a willingness to seek power and protection from One much greater than ourselves, to turn back to Him and to trust in His mercy. Without His help, America will not go forward.

I have a very special old Bible. And alongside a verse in the Second Book of Chronicles there are some words, handwritten, very faded by now. And, believe me, the person who wrote those words was an authority. Her name was Nelle Wilson Reagan. She was my mother. And she wrote about that verse, "A most wonderful verse for the healing of the nations."

Now, the verse that she'd marked reads: "If my people, which are called by my name, shall humble themselves, and pray, and seek my face, and turn from their wicked ways; then will I hear from heaven ... and will heal their land" (see 2 Chr 7:14).

I know that at times all of us—I do—feel that perhaps in our prayers we ask for too much. And then there are those other times when we feel that something isn't important enough to bother God with it. Maybe we should let Him decide those things.

The war correspondent Marguerite Higgins, who received the Pulitzer Prize for International Reporting because of her coverage of the Korean war, among all her writings had an account one day of the Fifth Company of marines who were part of an eighteen-thousand-man force that was in combat with a hundred thousand of the enemy. And she described an incident that took place early, just after dawn on a very cold morning. It was forty-two degrees below zero. And the weary marines, half frozen, stood by their dirty, mud-covered trucks, eating their breakfast from tin cans.

She saw one huge marine was eating cold beans with a trench knife. His clothes were frozen stiff as a board; his face was covered with a heavy beard and crusted with mud. And one of the little group of war correspondents who were on hand went up to him and said, "If I were God and could grant you anything you wished, what would you most like?" And the marine stood there for a moment, looking down at that cold tin of beans, and then he raised his head and said, "Give me tomorrow."

-Remarks at the annual National Prayer Breakfast,
February 3, 1983

The Bible's Influence on America

Of the many influences that have shaped the United States of America into a distinctive nation and people, none may be said to be more fundamental and enduring than the Bible.

Deep religious beliefs stemming from the Old and New Testaments of the Bible inspired many of the early settlers of our country, providing them with the strength, character, convictions, and faith necessary to withstand great hardship and danger in this new and rugged land. These shared beliefs helped forge a sense of common purpose among the widely dispersed colonies—a sense of community that laid the foundation for the spirit of nationhood that was to develop in later decades.

The Bible and its teachings helped form the basis for the Founding Fathers' abiding belief in the inalienable rights of the individual, rights which they found implicit in the Bible's teachings of the inherent worth and dignity of each individual. This same sense of man patterned the convictions of those who framed the English system of law inherited by our own nation, as well as the ideals set forth in the Declaration of

Independence and the Constitution.

For centuries the Bible's emphasis on compassion and love for our neighbor has inspired institutional and governmental expressions of benevolent outreach such as private charity, the establishment of schools and hospitals, and the abolition of slavery.

Many of our greatest national leaders—among them Presidents Washington, Jackson, Lincoln, and Wilson—have recognized the influence of the Bible on our country's development. The plainspoken Andrew Jackson referred to the Bible as no less than "the rock on which our Republic rests." Today our beloved America and, indeed, the world, is facing a decade of enormous challenge. As a people we may well be tested as we have seldom, if ever, been tested before. We will need resources of spirit even more than resources of technology, education, and armaments. There could be no more fitting moment than now to reflect with gratitude, humility, and urgency upon the wisdom revealed to us in the writing that Abraham Lincoln called "the best gift God has ever given to man.... But for it we could not know right from wrong."

-A proclamation, Year of the Bible, February 3, 1983

There's No Freedom Without Faith

Prayer has sustained our people in crisis, strengthened us in times of challenge, and guided us through our daily lives since the first settlers came to this continent. Our forebears came not for gold, but mainly in search of God and the freedom to worship in their own way.

We've been a free people living under the law, with faith in our Maker and in our future. I've said before that the most sublime picture in American history is of George Washington on his knees in the snow at Valley Forge. That image personifies a people who know that it's not enough to depend on our own courage and goodness; we must also seek help from God, our Father and Preserver.

Abraham Lincoln said once that he would be the most foolish man on this footstool we call Earth, if he thought for one minute he could fulfill the duties that faced him if he did not have the help of One who was wiser than all others.

The French philosopher Alexis de Tocqueville, visiting America a hundred and fifty years ago, marveled at Americans because they understood that a free people must also be a religious people. "Despotism," he wrote, "may be able to do without faith, but freedom cannot."

Today, prayer is still a powerful force in America, and our faith in God is a mighty source of strength. Our Pledge of Allegiance states that we are "one nation under God," and our currency bears the motto, "In God We Trust."

The morality and values such faith implies are deeply embedded in our national character. Our country embraces those principles by design, and we abandon them at our peril. Yet in recent years, well-meaning Americans in the name of freedom have taken freedom away. For the sake of religious tolerance, they've forbidden religious practice in our public classrooms. The law of this land has effectively removed prayer from our classrooms.

How can we hope to retain our freedom through the generations if we fail to teach our young that our liberty springs from an abiding faith in our Creator?

Thomas Jefferson once said, "Almighty God created the mind free." But current interpretation of our Constitution holds that the minds of our children cannot be free to pray to God in public schools. No one will ever convince me that a moment of voluntary prayer will harm a child or threaten a school or state. But I think it can strengthen our faith in a Creator who alone has the power to bless America.

One of my favorite passages in the Bible is the promise God gives us in Second Chronicles: "If my people, which are called by my name, shall humble themselves and pray and seek my face and turn from their wicked ways, then will I hear from heaven and will forgive their sin and will heal their land" (2 Chr 7:14).

That promise is the hope of America and of all our people.

Because of my faith in that promise, I'm particularly pleased to be able to tell you today that this administration will soon submit to the United States Congress a proposal to amend our Constitution to allow our children to pray in school. No one must ever be forced or coerced or pressured to take part in any religious exercise, but neither should the government forbid religious practice. The amendment we'll propose will restore the right to pray.

I thank you all for coming here today and for the good work that you do for our people, our country, and our God every day of the year. But I also hope that I can count on your help in the days and months ahead as we work for passage of this amendment.

Changing the Constitution is a mammoth task. It should never be easy. But in this case, I believe we can restore a freedom that our Constitution was always meant to protect. I have never believed that the oft-quoted amendment was supposed to protect us from religion. It was to protect religion from government tyranny.

Together, let us take up the challenge to reawaken America's religious and moral heart, recognizing that a deep and abiding faith in God is the rock upon which this great nation was founded.

-Remarks at a White House ceremony in observance of National Day of Prayer, May 1, 1982

The Bible Is the Inspired Word of God

Today America is in the midst of a spiritual revival. From the growth of your radio and television stations to the polls of George Gallup, we see the signs of Americans returning to God. On our campuses the political activism of the sixties has been replaced with the religious commitment of the eighties. Organizations like Campus Crusade for Christ, the Fellowship of Christian Athletes, and Youth for Christ have grown in popularity. And why not? Your message is rooted in one sure guide for life, the guide for our Founding Fathers and every generation of Americans as much as for ourselves, the infallible wellspring of our national goodness: the Bible, the inspired Word of God.

How ironic that even as America returns to its spiritual roots, our courts lag behind. They talk of our constitutional guarantee of religious liberty as if it meant freedom from religion, freedom from—actually a prohibition on—all values rooted in religion. Well, yes, the Constitution does say that "Congress shall make no law respecting an establishment of religion." But then it adds: "or prohibiting the free exercise thereof."

The First Amendment protects the rights of Americans to freely exercise their religious beliefs in an atmosphere of toleration and accommodation. As I have noted in the past, certain court decisions have, in my view, wrongly interpreted the First Amendment so as to restrict, rather than protect, individual rights of conscience. What greater legacy could we leave our children than a new birth of religious freedom in this one nation under God? Now, I hear the smart money in this town say we haven't got a prayer, but somehow I believe the Man upstairs is listening and that He'll show us how to return to America's schoolchildren the right that every member of Congress has: to begin each day with a simple, voluntary prayer.

At the heart of our Judeo-Christian ethic is a reverence for life. From the Ten Commandments to the Sermon on the Mount, the mission of faith is to cherish and magnify life—and through it God's holy name. Yet since the Supreme Court's decision in *Roe v. Wade,* there have been twenty million abortions in America. And this callousness for life can spill over into other areas, leading to decisions on who is good enough to live and who is not.

All we know about the human spirit contradicts this mechanistic, materialistic view of man. Perhaps you saw in the papers recently the story of a young Irish author, Christy Nolan, who has received one of Britain's most coveted literary awards, the Whitbread Book of the Year award. Some say he's the new James Joyce. Little, except talent, is extraordinary here—talent and the terrible fact that complications at birth left Christy Nolan totally paralyzed. He cannot walk, talk, or control his limbs. He writes using what he calls a unicorn stick attached to his forehead, pecking out the words on a typewriter, a page a day. In his message accepting the award, Christy Nolan wrote: "Imagine what I would have missed if the doctors had not revived me on that September day long ago."

Imagine what so many deemed unworthy of life have missed. Imagine what the rest of us have missed for their absence. Life and the human spirit are absolutes, indivisible. Isn't it time we returned the right to life to the core of our national values, our national customs, and our national laws?

Let me tell you one other story of Sandinista religious repression. I mentioned Campus Crusade for Christ earlier. In late 1985 the Crusade's national director for Nicaragua, Jimmy Hassan, was arrested. For hours, he was harassed, questioned, and put in a tiny cell, questioned again, placed in a cold room, questioned yet again, and had a gun put to his head and the trigger pulled. Thank goodness the gun was empty. The reason for all this: He had been preaching the gospel to young people. But that's not why I'm telling you his story. No, I thought you'd want to hear his account of what he said to one of his captors when, after hours of interrogation and humiliation, he was released: "I said to him I wanted to leave it clear that as a Christian I loved him, and I wanted him to know Christ."

Is there any force on Earth more powerful than that love? Is there any truth that gives more strength than knowing that God has a special plan for each one of us? Yes, man is sinful, separated from God. But there is God's promise of salvation, even for the least likely of us.

A few weeks ago I received a letter from a family in Wisconsin. The woman who wrote the letter is a widow, her husband was killed in World War II. They enclosed with the letter this prayer:

Hear me, O God; never in the whole of my lifetime have I spoken to You, but just now I feel like sending You my greetings.

You know, from childhood on, they've always told me You are not. I, like a fool, believed them.

I've never contemplated your creation, and yet tonight, gazing up out of my shell hole, I marveled at the shimmering stars above me and suddenly knew the cruelty of the lie.

Will You, my God, reach your hand out to me, I wonder? But I will tell You, and You will understand. Is it not strange that light should come upon me and I see You amid this night of hell?

And there is nothing else I have to say. This, though: I'm glad that I've learned to know You.

At midnight we are scheduled to attack. But You are looking on, and I am not afraid.

The signal. Well, I guess I must be going. I've been happy with You.

This more I want to say: As You well know, the fighting will be cruel, and even tonight I may come knocking at your door. Although I have not been a friend to You before, still, will You let me enter now, when I do come?

Why, I am crying, O God, my Lord. You see what happens to me: Tonight my eyes were opened.

Farewell, my God. I'm going and not likely to come back.

Strange, is it not, but death I fear no longer.

That young man did die in that attack, and that prayer was found on the body of a young Soviet soldier who was killed in that combat in 1944.

-Remarks at the Annual Convention of the National
Religious Broadcasters Association, February 1, 1983

10 | PRAYER AND NATIONAL PURPOSE

> How, with so much against them, could
> our Founding Fathers have dared so much,
> to declare for all the world and all future
> generations the rights of man, the dignity of
> the individual, the hopes of all humanity?
> Was it because they believed that God was
> on their side? Or was it because they prayed
> to discover how they might be on God's
> side? Our Founding Fathers knew that
> their hope was in prayer. – 1987

The Source of America's Strength

Our nation's motto—"In God We Trust"—was not chosen lightly. It reflects a basic recognition that there is a divine authority in the universe to which this nation owes homage.

Throughout our history Americans have put their faith in God and no one can doubt that we have been blessed for it. The earliest settlers of this land came in search of religious freedom. Landing on a desolate shoreline, they established a spiritual foundation that has served us ever since.

It was the hard work of our people, the freedom they enjoyed, and their faith in God that built this country and made it the envy of the world. In all of our great cities and towns evidence of the faith of our people is found: houses of worship of every denomination are among the oldest structures.

While never willing to bow to a tyrant, our forefathers were always willing to get to their knees before God. When catastrophe threatened, they turned to God for deliverance. When the harvest was bountiful the first thought was thanksgiving to God.

Prayer is today as powerful a force in our nation as it has ever been. We as a nation should never forget this source of strength. And while recognizing that the freedom to choose a godly path is the essence of liberty, as a nation we cannot but hope that more of our citizens would, through prayer, come into a closer relationship with their Maker.

-A proclamation, National Day of Prayer,
March 19, 1981

There's Hope in Prayer

Distinguished clergy and Senators and Congressmen, guests, all our good friends: Nancy and I are delighted to be here with you today. It gives one a very good feeling to see so many of our national leaders here, and so many representatives of other countries, gathering together in a community of faith. Two hundred years ago another group of statesmen gathered together in Philadelphia to revise the Articles of Confederation and bring forth our Constitution. They often found themselves at odds, their purpose lost in acrimony and self-interest, until Benjamin Franklin stood up and said: "I have lived a long time, and the longer I live, the more convincing proof I see of this truth—that God governs in the affairs of men. And if a sparrow cannot fall to the ground without His notice, is it probable that an empire can rise without His aid?" And then he called upon the convention to open each day with prayer.

How, with so much against them, could our Founding Fathers have dared so much, to declare for all the world and all future generations the rights of man, the dignity of the individual, the hopes of all humanity? Was it because they believed that God was on their side? Or was it because they prayed to discover how they might be on God's side? Our Founding Fathers knew that their hope was in prayer. And that's why our Declaration of Independence begins with an affirmation of faith and why our Congress opens every day with prayer. It is why the First Congress of the fledgling United States in the Northwest Ordinance provided for schools that would teach "religion, morality, and knowledge"—because they knew that no man, no nation, could grow in freedom without divine guidance.

If I might be allowed a personal note here: When I attended the commencement ceremonies at the Air Force Academy, I was surprised at how many of the graduating cadets came up to me, hand extended—930 in all—and told me they were praying for me. When I mentioned this to the commanding general, he told me that every morning you could find several hundred cadets in the chapel beginning their day with prayer. Hardly a day goes by that I'm not told—sometimes in letters and sometimes by people I meet—that they're praying for me. It's a warm but humbling feeling. Sometimes I answer when someone says that; I feel I have to say something. And I tell them that if they ever get a busy signal, it's because I'm in there ahead of them.

I know it's those prayers, and millions like them, that are building high and strong this cathedral of freedom that we call America; those prayers, and millions like them, that will always keep our country secure and make her a force for good in these too-troubled times. And that's why as a nation we must embrace our faith, for as long as we endeavor to do good—and we must believe that will be always—we will find our strength, our hope, and our true happiness in prayer and in the Lord's will.

-Remarks at the Annual National
Prayer Breakfast, February 5, 1987

The Right to Pray in Public

Calvin Coolidge, a president whom I greatly admire, once said, "The government of a country never gets ahead of the religion of a country." Fostering the faith and character of our people is one of the great trusts of responsible leadership. I deeply believe that if those in government offer a good example, and if the people preserve the freedom which is their birthright as Americans, no one need fear the future.

Unfortunately, in the last two decades we've experienced an onslaught of such twisted logic that if Alice were visiting America, she might think she'd never left Wonderland. We're told that it somehow violates the rights of others to permit students in school who desire to pray to do so. Clearly this infringes on the freedom of those who choose to pray—a freedom taken for granted since the time of our Founding Fathers.

This would be bad enough, but the purge of God from our schools went much farther. In one case, a federal court ruled against the right of children to voluntarily say grace before lunch in the school cafeteria. In another situation a group of children, again on their own initiative and with their parents' approval, wanted to begin the school day with a minute of prayer and meditation, and they, too, were prohibited from doing so. Students have even been prevented from having voluntary prayer groups on school property after class hours just on their own.

Now, no one is suggesting that others should be forced into any religious activity, but to prevent those who believe in God from expressing their faith is an outrage. And the relentless drive to eliminate God from our schools can and should be stopped.

This issue has brought people of goodwill and every faith together to make the situation right. We believe that permitting voluntary prayer in public schools is within the finest traditions of this country and consistent with the principles of American liberty. Neither the constitutional amendment that I've endorsed nor the legislative remedies offered by others permits anyone to be coerced into religious activity. Instead, these measures are designed to protect the rights of those who choose to pray as well as those who choose not to....

And today I'd like to take this opportunity to urge the Senate to move directly on the constitutional amendment now awaiting action. But Senate action is not enough. The leadership in the House has the proposed constitutional amendment bottled up and has, thus far, failed to hold the appropriate hearings. Some suggest we should keep religion out of politics. Well, the opposite is also true. Those in politics should keep their hands off of the religious freedom of our people, and especially our children.

Earlier I quoted Calvin Coolidge. He had some other words I'd like to share with you. "It would be difficult for me to conceive," President Coolidge said, "of anyone being able to administer the duties of a great office like the presidency without a belief in the guidance of Divine Providence. Unless the president is sustained by an abiding faith in the divine power, I cannot understand how he would have the courage to attempt to meet the various problems that constantly pour in upon him from all parts of the Earth."

Well, after twenty months I can attest to the truth of those words. Faith in God is a vital guidepost, a source of inspiration, and a pillar of strength in times of trial. In recognition of this, the Congress and the Supreme Court begin each day with a prayer, and that's why we provide chaplains for the armed forces. We can and must respect the rights of those who are nonbelievers, but we must not cut ourselves off from this indispensable source of strength and guidance.

I think it would be a tragedy for us to deny our children what the rest of us, in and out of government, find so valuable. If the president of the United States can pray with others in the Oval Office—and I have on a number of occasions—then let's make certain that our children have the same right as they go about preparing for their futures and for the future of this country.

-Remarks at a candle-lighting ceremony
for prayer in schools, September 25, 1982

Prayer and the American Spirit

Prayer is the mainspring of the American spirit, a fundamental tenet of our people since before the republic was founded. A year before the Declaration of Independence, in 1775, the Continental Congress proclaimed the first National Day of Prayer as the initial positive action they asked of every colonist.

Two hundred years ago in 1783, the Treaty of Paris officially ended the long, weary Revolutionary War, during which a National Day of Prayer had been proclaimed every spring for eight years. When peace came the National Day of Prayer was forgotten. For almost half a century, as the nation grew in power and wealth, we put aside this deepest expression of American belief—our national dependence on the providence of God.

It took the tragedy of the Civil War to restore a National Day of Prayer. As Abraham Lincoln said, "Intoxicated with unbroken success, we have become too self-sufficient to feel the necessity of redeeming and preserving grace, too proud to pray to the God that made us."

Revived as an annual observance by Congress in 1952, the National Day of Prayer has become a great unifying force for our citizens who come from all the great religions of the world. Prayer unites people. This common expression of reverence heals and brings us together as a nation, and we pray it may one day bring renewed respect for God to all the peoples of the world.

From General Washington's struggle at Valley Forge to the present, this nation has fervently sought and received divine guidance as it pursued the course of history. This occasion provides our nation with an opportunity to further recognize the source of our blessings, and to seek His help for the challenges we face today and in the future.

-A proclamation, National Day of Prayer,
January 27, 1984

Praying for Those in Need

We all in this room, I know, and we know many millions more everywhere, turn to God in prayer, believe in the power and the spirit of prayer. And yet so often, we direct our prayers to those problems that are immediate to us, knowing that He has promised His help to us when we turn to Him. And yet in a world today that is so torn with strife, where the divisions seem to be increasing, I wonder if we have ever thought about the greatest tool that we have—that power of prayer and God's help.

If you could add together the power of prayer of the people just in this room, what would be its megatonnage? And have we maybe been neglecting this and not thinking in terms of a broader basis in which we pray to be forgiven for the animus we feel toward someone in perhaps a legitimate dispute, and at the same time recognize that while the dispute will go on, we have to realize that that other individual is a child of God even as we are and is beloved by God, as we like to feel that we are?

-Remarks at the Annual National
Prayer Breakfast, February 22, 1984

When the Government Forbids Prayer

From the early days of the colonies, prayer in school was practiced and revered as an important tradition. Indeed, for nearly two hundred years of our nation's history, it was considered a natural expression of our religious freedom. But in 1962 the Supreme Court handed down a controversial decision prohibiting prayer in public schools.

Sometimes I can't help but feel the First Amendment is being turned on its head. Because ask yourselves: Can it really be true that the First Amendment can permit Nazis and Ku Klux Klansmen to march on public property, advocate the extermination of people of the Jewish faith and the subjugation of blacks, while the same amendment forbids our children from saying a prayer in school?

When a group of students at the Guilderland High School in Albany, New York, sought to use an empty classroom for voluntary prayer meetings, the Second Circuit of Appeals said no. The court thought it might be dangerous because students might be coerced into praying if they saw the football captain or student body president participating in prayer meetings.

Then there was the case of the kindergarten class reciting a verse before their milk and cookies. They said, "We thank you for the flowers so sweet. We thank you for the food we eat. We thank you for the birds that sing. We thank you, God, for everything." But a federal court of appeals ordered them to stop. They were supposedly violating the Constitution of the United States.

Teddy Roosevelt told us, "The American people are slow to wrath, but when their wrath is once kindled it burns like a consuming flame." Up to 80 percent of the American people support voluntary prayer. They understand what the Founding Fathers intended. The First Amendment of the Constitution was not written to protect the people from religion; that amendment was written to protect religion from government tyranny.

The amendment says, "Congress shall make no law respecting an establishment of religion or prohibiting the free exercise thereof." What could be more clear?

The act that established our public school system called for public education to see that our children learned about religion and morality. References to God can be found in the Mayflower Compact of 1620, the Declaration of Independence, the Pledge of Allegiance, and the National Anthem. Our legal tender states, "In God We Trust."

When the Constitution was being debated at the Constitutional Convention, Benjamin Franklin rose to say: "The longer I live, the more convincing proofs I see that God governs in the affairs of men. Without His concurring aid, we shall succeed in this political building no better than the builders of Babel." He asked: "Have we now forgotten this powerful Friend? Or do we imagine we no longer need His assistance?" Franklin then asked the Convention to begin its daily deliberations by asking for the assistance of Almighty God.

George Washington believed that religion was an essential pillar of a strong society. In his farewell address, he said, "Reason and experience both forbid us to expect that national morality can prevail in exclusion of religious principle." And when John Jay, the first Chief Justice of the United States Supreme Court, was asked in his dying hour if he had any farewell counsels to leave his children, Jay answered, "They have the Book."

But now we're told our children have no right to pray in school. Nonsense. The pendulum has swung too far toward intolerance against genuine religious freedom. It's time to redress the balance.

Former Supreme Court Justice Potter Stewart noted if religious exercises are held to be an impermissible activity in schools, religion is placed at an artificial and state-created disadvantage. Permission for such exercises for those who want them is necessary if the schools are truly to be neutral in the matter of religion. And a refusal to permit them is seen not as the realization of state neutrality, but rather as the establishment of a religion of secularism.

The Senate will soon vote on a constitutional amendment to permit voluntary vocal prayer in public schools. If two-thirds of the Senate approve, then we must convince the House leadership to permit a vote on the issue. I am confident that if the Congress passes our amendment this year, then the state legislatures will do likewise, and we'll be able to celebrate a great victory for our children.

Our amendment would ensure that no child be forced to recite a prayer. Indeed, it explicitly states this. Nor would the state be allowed to compose the words of any prayer. But the courts could not forbid our children from voluntary vocal prayer in their schools. And by reasserting their liberty of free religious expression, we will be helping our children understand the diversity of America's religious beliefs and practices.

If ever there was a time for you, the good people of this country, to make your voices heard, to make the mighty power of your will the decisive force in the halls of Congress, that time is now.

-Radio address, February 25, 1984

Prayer in Times of Crisis

Throughout our history, our leaders have always turned to prayer in times of crisis. All of us know how George Washington knelt in the snow at Valley Forge to ask for divine assistance when the fate of our nation hung in the balance. Abraham Lincoln issued a proclamation shortly after the battle of Gettysburg entreating the nation to pray for "perfect enjoyment of union and fraternal peace." And after the shock of Pearl Harbor, Franklin Roosevelt told us he took courage from the thought that "the vast majority of the members of the human race" joined us in a common prayer for victory as we fought for "liberty under God."

Prayer, of course, is deeply personal. Many of us have been taught to pray by people we love. In my case, it was my mother. I learned quite literally at her knee. My mother gave me a great deal, but nothing she gave me was more important than that special gift, the knowledge of the happiness and solace to be gained by talking to the Lord. The way we pray depends both on our religious convictions and our own individual dispositions, but the light of prayer has a common core. It is our hopes and our aspirations, our sorrows and fears, our deep remorse and renewed resolve, our thanks and joyful praise, and most especially our love, all turned toward a loving God. The Talmud calls prayer the "service of the heart," and St. Paul urged us to "pray without ceasing" (see 1 Thes 5:14).

Of course, it's important to remember that prayer doesn't always mean asking God to give us something. Prayer can also be a vehicle for worship—for recognition of the supreme reality, the reality of God and His love. Worshipful prayer seems especially appropriate in this holiday season, when in Hanukkah we celebrate God's faithfulness to the Jewish nation and in Christmas we mark the birth of One whom some honor as a great and holy prophet and others adore as the Son of God. Listen, if you will, for a moment to the words of the Scriptures:

> And there were in the same country shepherds abiding in the field, keeping watch over their flock by night. And, lo, the angel of the Lord came upon them, and the glory of the Lord shone round about them. And they were sore afraid. And the angel said unto them, "Fear not, for behold, I bring you good tidings of great joy, which shall be to all people. For unto you is born this day in the city of David a Savior, which is Christ the Lord. And this shall be a sign unto you. Ye shall find the babe wrapped in swaddling clothes, lying in a manger" (see Lk 2:8-14). And suddenly there was with the angel a multitude of the heavenly host praising God and saying, "Glory to God in the highest, and on earth peace, good will toward men."

Perhaps, in our own prayers we would do well to remember the words of the heavenly host on that one still night so long ago, each of us in our own way giving glory to God and asking in all earnestness for peace on Earth, and goodwill toward men.

-Remarks on signing the 1987 National Day of Prayer
Proclamation, December 22, 1986

Praying When Facing Adversity

In 1952 the Congress of the United States, resuming a tradition observed by the Continental Congress from 1776 to 1783 and followed intermittently thereafter, adopted a resolution calling on the president to set aside and proclaim a suitable day each year as a National Day of Prayer. At the time the resolution was adopted, Americans were dying on the battlefield in Korea. More than 125,000 of our young men had been killed or wounded in that conflict, the third major war in which our troops were involved in a century barely half over.

Members of Congress who spoke for the resolution made clear that they felt the nation continued to face the very same challenges that preoccupied our Founders: the survival of freedom in a world frequently hostile to human ideals and the struggle for faith in an age that openly doubted or vehemently denied the existence of the Almighty. One senator remarked that "it would be timely and appropriate for the people of our nation to join in this service of prayer in the spirit of the Founding Fathers who believed that God governs in the affairs of men and who based their Declaration of Independence upon a firm reliance on the protection of Divine Providence."

Human nature is such that times of distress, grief, and war—or their recent memory—impel us to acknowledgments we are often too proud to make, or too prone to forget, in periods of peace and prosperity. During the Civil War Lincoln said that he was driven to his knees in prayer because he was convinced that he had nowhere else to go. During World War II, an unknown soldier in a trench in Tunisia left behind a scrap of paper with the verses:

Stay with me, God. The night is dark,
The night is cold: my little spark
Of courage dies. The night is long;
Be with me, God, and make me strong.

America has lived through many a cold, dark night, when the cupped hands of prayer were our only shield against the extinction of courage. Though that flame has flickered from time to time, it burns brightest when we are willing, as we ought to be now, to turn our faces and our hearts to God not only at moments of personal danger and civil strife, but in the full flower of the liberty, peace, and abundance that He has showered upon us.

-A proclamation, National Day of Prayer,
December 22, 1986

The Joy of Knowing God

Last week, when the shuttle exploded, we hadn't, as a nation, had a tragedy like that that we actually witnessed as it happened. And as I watched the coverage on television, I thought of a poem that came out of a war. And it became literally the creed of America's fliers all over the world. I quoted a line from that poem when I spoke on TV the night of the tragedy. That poem was written by a young man named [John G.] Magee. He was nineteen years old, a volunteer in the Canadian Air Force. He was an American, but he'd gone there before our country was in the war. He was killed four days after Pearl Harbor, but he left something that does live on—that poem. It says:

Oh, I've slipped the surly bonds of earth and danced the skies on laughter-silvered wings.

Sunward I've climbed and joined the tumbling north of sun-split clouds and done a hundred things you have not dreamed of.

Wheeled and soared and swung high in the sunlit silence, hovering there I've chased the shouting wind along and flung my eager craft through footless halls of air—up, up to the long, delirious burning blue I've topped the windswept heights with easy grace, where never lark or even eagle flew.

And while with silent lifting mind, I've trod the high untrespassed sanctity of space, put out my hand and touched the face of God.

I used to think it was a poem about the joy of escaping gravity, but even more, it's a poem about joy. And God gave us joy; that was His gift to us. We've all been sad the past week, and yet there was something good about the way we wept together as we said goodbye and suddenly remembered that we are a family. And now the time has come to remember the words of the Bible, "Weeping may endure for a night, but joy cometh in the morning" (see Ps 30:5).

-Remarks at the Annual National
Prayer Breakfast, February 6, 1986

Loving God

All of us know of that wonderful individual, Mother Teresa, that living saint. If you've ever met Mother Teresa, you know what I mean. She's probably thrust into your hand a pamphlet telling you to love Christ. She wouldn't mind my saying that she's no longer young. If she were here she'd say, "Look who's talking." But she is no longer young, and she's not always well. But she's inexhaustible. You may have heard of her trip to Ethiopia at the height of the famine. She got there after a terribly long journey, but went without pause straight to a food distribution center. Thousands of those people crowded around her trying to touch her. She stood there and shook hands, ten thousand of them. And later she was asked, "How could you do that? Weren't you exhausted?" And she said, "It's my faith that feeds me."

Well, sometime back, a senator approached her when she was visiting Washington and said, "Mother, the problems of the world are so terrible and things look so bad, what can we do?" She said, "Love God." Different things impel different people. Mother Teresa is impelled by joy. She sings like a woman in love and she is—in love with God. She's a great example of the truth of a great paradox: that mankind can find freedom only in surrender, joy only in submission, wealth only in what we give away, and safety only in a promise—God's promise of life everlasting.

Mother Teresa shines with joy in spite of the fact that she spends so much of her time in the unhappiest places on this Earth. If you look at the world stage, you don't see a lot to make you glad, but in the midst of hellish circumstances—in Mexico after the earthquake, in Ethiopia during a famine, in

South Africa and Angola and Nicaragua—in all those painful places we still see joy, God's gift, and the energy that it gives.

There are perhaps three thousand of us here in this room—the wealthy and the powerful, those who've known neither wealth nor power. We have teachers here and diplomats, inmates from a local reformatory, captains of industry are here and so are just moms and dads and insurance salesmen and people that do things like that—such diverse lives. And yet we all have in common the usual problems of life, the usual difficulties. And we're trying to achieve some kind of happiness while, in the process, causing as little pain to others as possible. We have so much in common—we share an anchor that roots us in the heavy seas, and that anchor is the joy that God gave us. Let our thoughts today be of how man harnesses his sadness and turns it into triumphant work. And that's what I wish for all of us in this room—that in our individual work this year, we will fight on for what's right and good and resist the badness that is in us and that we'll do it with joy, because God gave that as a gift to be used.

-Remarks at the Annual National
Prayer Breakfast, February 6, 1986

Prayer in American History

Prayer is deeply woven into the fabric of our history from its very beginnings. The same Continental Congress that declared our independence also proclaimed a National Day of Prayer. And from that time forward, it would be hard to exaggerate the role that prayer has played in the lives of individual Americans and in the life of the nation as a whole.

Our greatest leaders have always turned to prayer at times of crisis. We recall the moving story of George Washington kneeling in the snow at Valley Forge to ask for divine assistance when the fate of our fledgling nation hung in the balance. And Abraham Lincoln tells us that on the eve of the Battle of Gettysburg, "I went into my room and got down on my knees in prayer." Never before, he added, had he prayed "with as much earnestness."

More than once, Lincoln also summoned the entire nation to its knees before the God in whose hand lies the destiny of nations. It was, he said, "fit and becoming in all peoples, at all times, to acknowledge and revere the Supreme Government of God ... and to pray with all fervency and contrition...."

Accordingly, like the presidents who have come before me, I invite my fellow citizens to join me in earnest prayer that the God who has led and protected us through so many trials and favored us with such abundant blessings may continue to watch over our land. Let us never forget the wise counsel of Theodore Roosevelt that "all our extraordinary material development ... will go for nothing unless with that growth goes hand in hand with the moral, the spiritual growth that will enable us to use aright the other as in an instrument."

In prayer, let us ask that God's fight may illuminate the minds and hearts of our people and our leaders, so that we may meet the challenges that lie before us with courage and wisdom and justice. In prayer let us recall with confidence the promise of old that if we humble ourselves before God and pray and seek His face, He will surely hear and forgive and heal and bless our land.

-A proclamation, National Day of Prayer,
January 18, 1986

Our Shared Faith in God

More than any other nation, ours draws inspiration from the creeds of many peoples from many parts of the world. They came to our shores from different ports of origin at different times in our history. But all of them—from the men and women who celebrated the first Thanksgiving more than three and a half centuries ago, to the boat people of Southeast Asia—came here with prayers on their lips and faith in their hearts.

It's because of this shared faith that we've become, in the words of the Pledge of Allegiance, "one nation under God, indivisible, with liberty and justice for all."

At every crucial turning point in our history Americans have faced and overcome great odds, strengthened by spiritual faith. The Plymouth settlers triumphed over hunger, disease, and a cruel northern wilderness because, in the words of William Bradford, "They knew they were pilgrims. So they committed themselves to the will of God and resolved to proceed."

George Washington knelt in prayer at Valley Forge and in the darkest days of our struggle for independence said that "the fate of unborn millions will now depend, under God, on the courage and conduct of this army."

Thomas Jefferson, perhaps the wisest of our Founding Fathers, had no doubt about the source from which our cause was derived. "The God who gave us life," he declared, "gave us liberty...."

And nearly a century later, in the midst of a tragic and at times seemingly hopeless Civil War, Abraham Lincoln vowed "that this nation, under God, shall have a new birth of freedom."

It's said that prayer can move mountains. Well, it's certainly moved the hearts and minds of Americans in their times of trial and helped them to achieve a society that, for all its imperfections, is still the envy of the world and the last, best hope of mankind.

And just as prayer has helped us as a nation, it helps us as individuals. In nearly all our lives, there are moments when our prayers and the prayers of our friends and loved ones help to see us through and keep us on the right path. In fact, prayer is one of the few things in this world that hurts no one and sustains the spirit of millions.

The Founding Fathers felt this so strongly that they enshrined the principle of freedom of religion in the First Amendment of the Constitution. The purpose of that amendment was to protect religion from the interference of government and to guarantee, in its own words, "the free exercise of religion."

-Radio address to the nation on prayer,
September 18, 1982

THE MAN FROM GALILEE

> Can you name one problem that would not be solved if we had simply followed the teachings of the man from Galilee? – 1967

In the Name of Christ

This power of prayer can be illustrated by a story that goes back to the fourth century. The Asian monk living in a little remote village, spending most of his time in prayer or tending the garden from which he obtained his sustenance—I hesitate to say the name because I'm not sure I know the pronunciation, but let me take a chance. It was Telemachus, back in the fourth century. And then one day, he thought he heard the voice of God telling him to go to Rome. And believing that he had heard, he set out. And weeks and weeks later, he arrived there, having traveled most of the way on foot.

And it was at a time of a festival in Rome. They were celebrating a triumph over the Goths. And he followed a crowd into the Colosseum, and then there in the midst of this great crowd, he saw the gladiators come forth, stand before the emperor, and say, "We who are about to die salute you." And he realized they were going to fight to the death for the entertainment of the crowds. And he cried out, "In the name of

Christ, stop!" And his voice was lost in the tumult there in the great Colosseum.

And as the games began, he made his way down through the crowd and climbed over the wall and dropped to the floor of the arena. Suddenly the crowds saw this scrawny little figure making his way out to the gladiators and saying, over and over again, "In the name of Christ, stop." And they thought it was part of the entertainment, and at first they were amused. But then, when they realized it wasn't, they grew belligerent and angry. And as he was pleading with the gladiators, "In the name of Christ, stop," one of them plunged his sword into his body. And as he fell to the sand of the arena in death, his last words were, "In the name of Christ, stop."

And suddenly, a strange thing happened. The gladiators stood looking at this tiny form lying in the sand. A silence fell over the Colosseum. And then, someplace up in the upper tiers, an individual made his way to an exit and left, and others began to follow. And in the dead silence, everyone left the Colosseum. That was the last battle to the death between gladiators in the Roman Colosseum. Never again did anyone kill or did men kill each other for the entertainment of the crowd.

One tiny voice that could hardly be heard above the tumult. "In the name of Christ, stop." It is something we could be saying to each other throughout the world today.

-Remarks at the Annual National
Prayer Breakfast, February 22, 1984

The Hands of Christ

I'd like to conclude with a story that is told by Dr. Paul Brand, the noted leprosy specialist, in his book *Fearfully and Wonderfully Made*. Dr. Brand tells us of how, after World War II, a group of German students—young people—volunteered to help rebuild a cathedral in England that had been a casualty of the *Luftwaffe* bombings. And as the work progressed, debate broke out on how best to restore a large statue of Jesus with his arms outstretched and bearing the familiar inscription: Come Unto Me. Careful patching could repair all damage to the statue except for Christ's hands, which had been destroyed by bomb fragments. Should they attempt the delicate task of reshaping those hands? And finally the young workers reached a decision that still stands today. The statue of Jesus has no hands, but the inscription now reads: Christ Has No Hands But Ours. Isn't that really what He was always trying to tell us? Trying to tell us that we must be the hands, as we've heard so eloquently here by so many already today.

-Remarks at the Annual National
Prayer Breakfast, February 5, 1987

Walking With Christ

I would like to tell just a little story. It was given to me by a friend on a printed card, author unknown. Now, I don't know how widely this has been distributed, or whether some of you or many of you are aware of it. I'm going to tell it anyway.

This unknown author wrote of a dream and in the dream was

walking down the beach beside the Lord. And as they walked, above him in the sky was reflected each stage and experience of his life. Reaching the end of the beach, and of his life, he turned back and looked back down the beach and saw the two sets of footprints in the sand, except that he looked again and realized that every once in awhile there was only one set of footprints. And each time there was only one set of footprints, it was when the experience reflected in the sky was one of despair, of desolation, of great trial or grief in his life.

And he turned to the Lord and said, "You said that if I would walk with You, You would always be beside me and take my hand. Why did You desert me? Why are You not there in my times of greatest need?" And the Lord said, "My child, I did not leave you. Where you see only one set of footprints, it was there that I carried you."

Abraham Lincoln once said, "I would be the most foolish person on this footstool Earth if I believed for one moment that I could perform the duties assigned to me without the help of One who is wiser than all." I know that in the days to come and the years ahead there are going to be many times when there will only be one set of footprints in my life. If I did not believe that, I could not face the days ahead.

-Remarks at the Annual National
Prayer Breakfast, February 5, 1981

The Christ Child

Some have suggested that in today's world, the family has somehow become less important. Well, I can't help thinking just the opposite: that when so much around us is whispering the little lie that we should live only for the moment and for ourselves, it's more important than ever for our families to affirm an older and more lasting set of values. Yet, for all that, in recent decades the American family has come under virtual attack. It has lost authority to government rule writers. It has seen its central role in the education of young people narrowed and distorted. And it's been forced to turn over to big government far too many of its own resources in the form of taxation.

Even so, the family today remains the fundamental unit of American life. But statistics show that it has lost ground, and I don't believe there's much doubt that the American family could be, and should be, much, much stronger. Just last month, I received a report on this from my Working Group on the Family, providing recommendations for giving the family new strength. Our administration will be giving these recommendations serious consideration in the days ahead. But for now we might all do well to keep our families in mind, to make certain that we don't take them for granted. For perhaps at no other time of the year are we able to enjoy our families so thoroughly, or see so clearly their importance to ourselves and our country.

And let us remember that in the midst of all the happy bustle of the season there is a certain quietness, a certain calm: the calm of one still night long ago and of a family—father, mother, and newborn child.

Now, some revere Christ as just a great prophet. Others worship Him as the Son of God. But to all, this season in which we mark His birth is indeed a time of glad tidings. So, in the midst of our celebrations, let us remember that one holy family in a manger on that still night in Bethlehem so long ago and give renewed thanks for the blessings of our own families. And, yes, let us pray for "peace on earth, good will toward men...."

-Radio address, December 20, 1986

The Love of Jesus

Our mission stretches far beyond our borders; God's family knows no borders. In your life you face daily trials, but millions of believers in other lands face far worse. They are mocked and persecuted for the crime of loving God. To every religious dissident trapped in that cold, cruel existence, we send our love and support. Our message? You are not alone; you are not forgotten; do not lose your faith and hope because someday you, too, will be free.

If the Lord is our light, our strength, and our salvation, whom shall we fear? Of whom shall we be afraid? No matter where we live, we have a promise that can make all the difference, a promise from Jesus to soothe our sorrows, heal our hearts, and drive away our fears. He promised there will never be a dark night that does not end. Our weeping may endure for a night, but joy cometh in the morning. He promised if our hearts are true, His love will be as sure as sunlight. And, by dying for us, Jesus showed how far our love should be ready to go: all the way.

"For God so loved the world that He gave His only begotten Son, that whosoever believeth in Him, should not perish but have everlasting life" (see Jn 3:16). I'm a little self-conscious because I know very well you all could recite that verse to me.

Helping each other, believing in Him, we need never be afraid. We will be part of something far more powerful, enduring, and good than all the forces here on Earth. We will be a part of paradise.

-Remarks, Annual Convention of the National
Religious Broadcasters, January 30, 1984

What America Believes

We're an optimistic people. We inherited a vast land of endless skies, tall mountains, rich fields, and open prairies. It made us see the possibilities in everything. It made us hopeful. And we devised an economic system that rewarded individual effort, that gave us good reason for hope. We love peace. We hate war. We think—and always have—that war is a great sin, a woeful waste. We wish to be at peace with our neighbors. We want to live in harmony with our friends. There is one other part of our national character I wish to speak of. Religion and faith are very important to us. We're a nation of many religions. But most Americans derive their religious belief from the Bible of Moses, who delivered a people from slavery; the Bible of Jesus Christ, who told us to love thy neighbor as thyself, to do unto your neighbor as you would have him do unto you. And this, too, formed us. It is why we wish well for others. It's why it grieves us when we hear of people who cannot live up to their full potential and who cannot live in peace.

- Remarks at Fudan University,
Shanghai, China, April 30, 1984